MEN WHO
RIDE MOUNTAINS

Men Who Ride Mountains

Incredible True Tales of Legendary Surfers

Peter Dixon

THE LYONS PRESS

Guilford, Connecticut
An imprint of The Globe Pequot Press

To Pahl, Jamie, and Megan . . . who grow by the sea

The Lyons Press is an imprint of The Globe Pequot Press.

Printed in Canada

2 4 6 8 10 9 7 5 3 1

Originally published by Bantam Books, Inc.

The Library of Congress Cataloging-in-Publication Data
is available on file.

ISBN 1-58574-388-7

Acknowledgments

Appreciation is extended to surfers everywhere who helped make this book possible. Special thanks go to Fred Van Dyke who made his unpublished notes available. The cooperation extended by Bob Cooper, John Fain, Ricky Grigg, and Craig Lockwood was invaluable. And finally my deep appreciation to Sali Dixon for countless hours of help and encouragement.

Thanks are due to the following photographers, whose work is credited on the pages indicated:
3, Judy Rohlof, Dixon collection; 6, Dixon collection; 9, Dr. Don James, Dixon collection; 14, P. L. Dixon; 17, P. L. Dixon; 23, P. L. Dixon; 37, Dixon collection; 41, P. L. Dixon; 47, P. L. Dixon; 55, photographer unknown, Dixon collection; 64, Dr. Don James; 70, Dr. Don James; 81, P. L. Dixon; 88, Ron Church; 97, Dr. Don James; 102, Judy Rohlof, Dixon collection; 112, P. L. Dixon; 117, Eric Thornberg; 119, Alby Falzon, Dixon collection; 124, P. L. Dixon; 132, Sali Dixon; 135, Ron Perrott, Dixon collection; 138, Dixon collection; 143, P. L. Dixon; 145, P. L. Dixon; 153, P. L. Dixon; 157, P. L. Dixon; 163, Leroy Grannis; 166, Dixon collection.

Contents

Introduction to the New Edition

An untold number of waves have been ridden by millions of surfers since MEN WHO RIDE MOUNTAINS was first published. That's a lot of great rides on something so simple as a wind-generated fun machine. The storm swells that roll for the coasts of our planet to feel the drag of the ocean's bottom and become surf create our sport—and the playing fields where big-wave riders challenge some of the most perilous forces of nature.

This new edition honors the pioneers of surfing. Their time was an era of purity before television and commercialism. Surfers were comrades then, driven to ride waves for the sake of simple, yet challenging adventure. Many paddled out to face awesome breaks that no one had ridden before. They traveled widely, exploring distant shores, always hoping to find and ride that perfect wave. And it was especially dangerous before the days of surf leashes and lifeguards who fly aboard helicopters to the rescue of a stranded surfer.

Many changes have occurred in surfing since the 1960s. Boards grew shorter, the style of surfing more radical. Then long boards returned and some grace came back to the sport. Boards are lighter today—highly refined. Most have three fins. Surfing has become an international sport beating on the doors of the Olympic Committee for inclusion.

Localism and aggression have become problems. The surf leash has allowed less-than-strong swimmers to participate. Big-wave surfers are being towed by powered Wave Runners into giant offshore breaks. Surfing's youth image has spawned hundreds of commercial enterprises and made millionaires of many. Private surfing camps draw high-paying guests, and professional surfing champions become well-rewarded media heroes.

What has not changed are the waves, except where development of harbors and beach homes have destroyed certain surfing breaks. Surfers have been uniting to battle these relentless enemies, and the polluters who poison the seas. Many of the pioneers lead the fight.

Riding a clean, fast-moving wave creates such profound physical and emotional satisfaction that hardly anything else surpasses this exuberant, challenging experience. Despite time and change, surfing is still a sport that only requires a board, guts, and skill. That's why the passion to surf continues to draw the young and keep the aged paddling out for one more wave.

Most of those whom I knew and wrote about in the first edition are still surfing, though a few have died, and are hopefully sliding heaven-sent waves in spirit. Many found a profession and fulfilling lifestyle in surfing. All of them were people who lived life to the extreme and made a contribution to surfing's rich heritage. Where are these men who ride mountains today, and what are they doing? Here's what's known about some of them:

- EDDIE AIKAU was lost at sea. When the ocean voyaging canoe he was crewing on overturned, Eddie attempted to paddle ashore for help. He was never seen again. The Eddie Aikau Big-Wave Classic surf contest is held each year in his honor.

- BEN AIPA has become one of the most respected board shapers in Hawaii. His son Akila has grown into a contest-winning competitive surfer.

- José Angle was a teacher and died diving black coral off Molokai. He was driven to push the limits and went too deep.

- Lance Carson lives in Los Angeles and works in the surfing industry. The surfboards and clothing that carry his name sell well, especially in Japan. Lance is one of the founders of "Surfrider Foundation," an effective, ocean-related environmental organization.

- Peter Cole, now a retired teacher, resides on Oahu, surfs big waves, and remains one of the most respected watermen ever to ride a surfboard. His enduring ability to judge and ride big waves has ensured his survival in the surf. He has become an activist for ocean environment protection.

- Bob Cooper is another Californian who found roots and fine waves in Australia. He's building boards there and surfing in local contests.

- Corky Carroll, one of the first to make surfing a career, lives in Seaside, California. He remains very active in the sport. Corky surfs in longboard contests, does television commercials, is a tennis pro, and manages a surf shop in Huntington Beach.

- Claude Codgin returned to Florida, where he shapes boards in the classic longboard tradition.

- Pat Curren lives in Cabo San Lucas, Mexico. Pat, the master shaper, still builds an occasional big-wave balsa wood board.

- Mickey Dora, the legendary mystery man, is rumored to be living at Jeffrey's Bay, South Africa. He is occasionally seen surfing at Biarritz, France, and Bell's Beach, Australia, drawing a crowd of curious admirers.

- GEORGE DOWNING, a pioneer surfer and surf contest promoter, is also involved in Hawaiian environmental issues. He's also a leader in native Hawaii causes.

- JOHNNY FAIN sells real estate in Malibu and is doing well after a hip replacement. He rides for the Becker Surfboard team in Master's surf meets.

- BERNARD "MIDGET" FARRELLY resides in Australia and manufactures foam surfboard blanks. He was the first world champion and has been a positive and articulate force in the sport ever since.

- RICKY GRIGG, freelance oceanographer and big-wave surfer, continues his scientific career in Hawaii, always finding time to ride when the north shore breaks.

- JEFF HACKMAN lives comfortably on Kauai and runs Quiksilver Europe sports clothes. He recently wrote his autobiography, *Mr. Sunset*, and surfs frequently with much of the skill of his younger days.

- FRED HEMMINGS entered politics, won local offices, and fought an unsuccessful election campaign to become governor of Hawaii. Fred still surfs the North Shore.

- RUSTY MILLER resides in Byron Bay, Australia. He is involved in the Internet, promotes tourism, farms, surfs frequently, and lives an organic lifestyle.

- BOB MCTAVISH also lives at Byron Bay with his family, in sight of the surf he loves. Bob continues to design and build innovative surfboards.

- MICKEY MUNOZ's skill as a surfboard shaper/builder is very much in demand. His surfing style inspires the young today.

- JOHN PECK lives in the Costa Mesa (California) area, still surfs with his fluid grace, restores classic surfboards, and has settled into a comfortable though reclusive way of life.

- PETE PETERSON died of a heart attack aboard his boat. He was an active surfer and diver and ran his successful salvage business until the end.

- FELIPÉ POMAR lives on the North Shore, sells real estate, and still rides the big surf on a longboard.

- JOCK SUTHERLAND works as a roofer, is famous for his avocado pies, and continues to win in master's surfing contests.

- BUZZY TRENT lives a reclusive life near Honolulu, where he works managing an estate. After a severe hang-gliding accident, he was forced to give up surfing.

- BRUCE VALLUZI died in 1995 on his way back from a surfing trip in South Africa. He was the first East Coast surfer to master Hawaii's north shore waves and win the respect of big-wave riders.

- NAT YOUNG, who more than anyone brought about the short board revolution, lives in Australia and continues to be a respected spokesperson for the surfing way of life.

- FRED VAN DYKE, a retired teacher, and his wife, Joan Marie, alternate between Montana and Hawaii lifestyles. Surfing, swimming, and hiking every day keep the Van Dykes young. Fred has recently authored a pair of young readers' books with surfing backgrounds.

and

- DON JAMES's photography, more than anyone else's, captured the true spirit and adventure of surfing. Don's remarkable photos appeared on every cover of my surfing books. We who surf owe him an everlasting thanks for his skill and artistry. Don died in December of 1997.

—Peter Dixon, 2001

MEN WHO
RIDE MOUNTAINS

CHAPTER 1

Men Who Ride Mountains

Across Oahu, a world away from tourist-trampled Honolulu, lies a length of beach surfers have come to call the North Shore. In the surfer's world this thirty-mile stretch of coastline represents Mount Olympus. This is the beach where the kings and queens of waves arrive to shatter themselves above the coral reefs in white-maned explosions. And these are the waves that draw the international surfing set, who jet in each winter to ride the moving mountains of the North Shore. Of the million or more surfers, only a few hundred have developed the skill and guts needed to ride the giants of Waimea Bay, Sunset Beach, or the blasting shorebreak at the Banzai Pipeline.

Surfers measure huge winter surf not in feet, but in units of fear. It was Peter Cole, pioneer North Shore big-wave rider, who created the concept of fear units as a measure of wave height. Wave height is difficult to determine. It's what the wave does to the surfer and the surfer with the wave that counts. To some, a relaxed five-foot breaker becomes huge and scary, while to others—like Cole and Greg Noll and Ricky Grigg—waves are huge and frightening only when they lose control.

Control is everything in big-wave surfing—and when you're out of control the wave usually wins. This control factor separates the men from the boys, and the North Shore surfer from the ordinary beach-break rider.

Come winter in Hawaii, the North Shore draws hun-

1

dreds of surfers who fly in to match their skill against the thundering surf. A few actually paddle past the shore-break and take off on these moving mountains of water. On their first few rides they usually go over the falls—wipe out. Then something happens to these few—they will them-selves to stay erect. They master the wave and make it across the collapsing face, and on to the safety of the wave's shoulder.

Some of the new arrivals experience such fear from their first big wave wipe-out that they return home or retire to less awesome surf. Some spend the rest of the season in-wardly cursing their bad luck, lack of courage, or whatever caused them to fail the challenge.

A few are injured after a blasting wipe-out. Some surf-ers from the milder, almost tranquil waves of California or Florida take one look at the heavies and wisely remain on the beach. Among big-wave surfers, there's no disgrace in avoiding waves you can't handle. They'd rather have it that way. One inexperienced man out of control can cause the rest of the plunging riders to wipe out, to go down amid a churning log jam of hurtling, spear-pointed surf-boards.

The men who ride Waimea Bay, Sunset Beach, or the Banzai Pipeline are not natural-born big-wave surfers. They've all gone through a surfer's apprenticeship—years of paddling and shattering wipe-outs. Most of these men were competitive swimmers or lifeguards, and most have a keen appreciation for the power of the surf they combat. Most are in their early thirties, a few are forty, and a hand-ful are a graying, balding fifty plus. Very few teen-agers ride the North Shore. They lack the maturity and experi-ence to surf the giants. When a teen-ager does, he's re-spected by his elders and treated like a man.

The North Shore is both a location and an attitude. The people who surf there come in two varieties—those who ride the giants, and the hot-dogging performers who surf with a flashy style on big waves. The hot-dogger looks for waves that are smooth, with well-defined curving shoulders under fifteen feet, while the true big-wave rider will take off on any wave—if there's a chance to survive. Each group finds its choice on the North Shore.

A perfection wave tunnels over at the Banzai Pipeline. John Peck races the break to find grandeur in the surf. (Judy Rohlof, Dixon collection)

Today's North Shore surfers are a bit like the knighted dragon-slayers of old, the barnstormers of the 1920's, the deering-do grand prix drivers, or that strange breed of free-falling sky divers. Some of these surfers appear to be Mr. Average Man; others are exceptional people who do brilliant, creative work when dry.

There are also a handful of pros, making a good living from linking their big-wave exploits to surfboard building, movie-making, and photography. Others come to establish a reputation. If a surfer can ride the North Shore and appear in the surfing magazines, there's a good chance he can later appear in a film, or be offered sponsorship by a board builder, or even model for well-paying advertisements. There's profit as well as glory on the North Shore.

Haleiwa, the sleepy capital of the North Shore, just shrugs during the annual winter invasion of surfers. The pinball games collect a few more coins, the Sea View Inn jams with surfers wanting dollar-and-a-half Japanese tempura, and the two grocery stores stock up on frozen TV dinners, cheap, fatty hamburger meat, and beer.

Life on the North Shore comes easy. Six or seven surfers crowd into a hundred-dollar-a-month shack. There's a movie in Haleiwa which shows Japanese films half the time and old westerns and sexy movies the other half, and admission is cheap. Surfers love the *samurai* flicks and whenever their hero Toshiro Mifune slashes his sword through a dozen bandits, the wave riders cheer for more.

The real heart of North Shore social life lies right across the Kamehameha Highway from big-wave Sunset Beach. The little store, post office, laundromat, coffee shop run by Mrs. Cammie and her husband becomes the hut, the meeting place, for most of the winter crew. Mrs. Cammie knows all the surfers, takes care of their mail, sends out fast messages that someone's draft notice has arrived, or that another surfer has received his G.I. Bill check from the government, or his tax refund. Cammie's store is where you'll find all the greats stoking up on hot chili and rice balls, washing their salt-encrusted blue jeans and sweatshirts, or posting a letter home asking for just a few dollars to eat on.

But when the surf comes up big and strong, there's no

time for laundromats, only time for the avalanche-like swells that come pounding in from the north. Then the "up-and-downers" arrive, the surfers in cars who prowl up and down the "Kam" Highway searching for the best break, looking for perfection waves the others haven't yet found. From day to day, even hour to hour, surf conditions change. When Waimea Bay starts cracking over at twenty feet, word spreads fast and the first men out have the best of it.

The first up quietly slip down to the Banzai Pipeline in hopes that the fastest, hollowest, tunneling waves of the North Shore will be breaking. If the Pipeline is makable and not too large, the hot-doggers and "goofy-footers" (surfers who ride left-footed) have a day of glory. The Banzai Pipeline has earned a reputation for the ghastliest, most blasting wipe-outs on the North Shore. Heads have been split wide open and bodies horribly cut by the sharp coral that awaits a surfer crunched in the vicious shore-break.

Grab a surfboard and paddle out. Let's meet a few of the wildest, gutsiest characters ever to slide across the face of a moving mountain of water. Outside the surfline, sitting on their "big guns" and waiting for the swells to become surf, are the kings of the waves.

The first surfer to take off on the biggest wave of the day goes by the name of "The Bull," Mr. Greg Noll of Hermosa Beach, California, builder of fine surfboards. Sliding down the crest of a twenty-five footer, 270-pound Noll looks like a pigmy in striped trunks. Dropping in right behind him and pushing for a good position comes Felipe Pomar, Peruvian champion and one of the few who dare to share a wave with Noll.

Paddling out to face the incoming Pomar and Noll comes Bruce Valluzzi, fresh from the two-foot shorebreaks of Florida. Bruce sees two human express trains barreling down on him and desperately paddles to escape the breaking wave that already begins to curl and crack over him. The wave closes out and Noll and Pomar make it past the crest, but Bruce is buried. The Florida boy's board is ripped from his hands and flung fifteen feet in the air. Bruce is driven ten feet down into the churning tons of

One of the first photos of Oahu, North Shore big-wave surfing. This was Makaha in 1953. Scoop Tzuki's photo inspired a generation of surfers to migrate to Hawaii.

(Dixon collection)

falling water. Bruce makes it to the surface and begins the long swim back to shore for his board. Later he'll go out and ride beautifully. Now he knows the waves won't kill, but only frighten and exhaust him.

Sitting outside the break where the early sun warms his back and lulls his senses is Mickey Dora—a legend, an enigma, the terror of California's Malibu surf. Dora will catch a few, ride flawlessly, and return to sit in the sun and watch the world from his position of isolation a half mile from shore.

Close to where the waves break, holding a critical position, is Ricky Grigg, carefully judging each break, waiting for the perfect wave. Ricky, a scientist from Scripps Institution of Oceanography, applies his academic background to the sport of surfing. Ricky, the intellectual with a sense of humor and intense competitive spirit, rides the heavies with a crisp precision that keeps him close to the break, the curl of each wave.

On the shore filming the action are the surfing-magazine photographers and the surf-film makers. Behind the long telephoto, Greg MacGillivary exposes miles of film for his surf epic *Free and Easy*. The surfers know Greg's filming, and the commercially-minded, hoping-to-be-a-movie-star surfers press a little harder, take greater chances. A great ride captured on film is their route to a surfer's immortality.

Arriving late will be the Australian gang, led by former world champion Nat Young. Aussies Bernard "Midget" Farrelly and Bob McTavish will be carrying their radical short boards, so fast turning that only surfers of excellence can possibly ride them. The short board Australian-style is all part of the movement to get closer to the break, become one with the wave, share its power, and come as close as possible to the wave's collapsing watery maw. Many Australians, big-wave riders, are hung up with the surfing mystique and ponder long hours after the sun has gone on the meaning of life, the surf, the power of the ocean. A few Aussies have gone far beyond the recreational aspect of surfing and have found a religion, a faith, a philosophy in the waves. Some non-surfers call them surfing's hippies, but they wear no uniform, and follow no party line. They

Fred Van Dyke, big-wave pioneer, powers down a Sunset Beach, Oahu giant.
(Dr. Don James, Dixon collection)

just surf beautifully, so in tune with the wave that for a brief instant . . . POW . . . they are one with the sea. And this closeness makes surfers wonder about life and nature and what is good and right in the world.

The North Shore—that's where it's happening. That's where the men who ride mountains gather; and that's where the northern swells, the best nature-made waves in the world, come rolling in—at Sunset Beach, the Pipeline, Waimea Bay—to lure a small army of board-carrying surfers to Hawaii each winter. Nowhere else in the world does this happen so fiercely, so compellingly.

There are other North Shores, other marvelous wave-riding areas where this mystique, this addiction to mastering the wave draws the big-wave riders. Wherever big waves break around the shores of this world, surfers are gathering. First they arrive as a single individual with board under arm. Then the word goes out . . . There's surf off Mexico's Cedros Island . . . Portugal's South Coast starts breaking in September . . . La Barre, near Biarritz, has the fastest left slide in Europe . . . Guam takes a north swell and can hold fifteen feet . . . They're stoked in Japan, getting ten feet off Chiba . . . Dewey found a bitchen' new spot off Costa Rica . . . And so it goes, as surfing becomes the fastest-growing sport in the world today.

And surfing has its divisions—like the pros, the classic stylists, the Australian method, the old-timers' straight-up-and-down stance. Surfing has developed into such a complex sport in the past ten years that it's almost impossible to define, to categorize, or to stereotype. What goes on in Australia is quite different from surfing in California. English surfers follow the lead set by the Australians, while French board riders play it cool and go their own leisurely way. Nowhere else, except in Peru, has a breed of gentlemen surfers developed. The French and Peruvians wouldn't think of surfing in the morning until they have had their coffee and rolls, or into the late afternoon, missing apéritif or cocktail time.

The North Shore idea is really an attitude, a feel for riding the heavies, a need to suffer blasting wipe-outs from collapsing watery giants, and a desire to push toward the limits of human capability. North Shores are everywhere the surfer goes to ride the big waves. Australia, Peru, South Africa, even France and California have their North Shores, their big surf days, and their share of men who ride mountains.

Where did it all begin? Who were the first of this strange and wild gang who set out to use the power of a nature-made wave for their own pleasure? Surfing is very old, as we shall see, but modern board-riding began at the start of our century. The pioneers, like Duke Kahanamoku, Lorrin Harrison, Pete Peterson and others, shouldn't be forgotten. They were the first ones to paddle out on the old, solid, long boards. They pointed the way for the big-wave riders of the 1950's and the current young crop of performing stylists.

The Duke is gone now and the other pioneers will follow him in years to come. So let us begin by journeying back to 1900, and see what it was like to surf on a big-swell day at Waikiki when not a single hotel or bar crowded the beach-front. Let us go back to when Duke and Dad Center took off on a screaming twenty-five footer to begin what was to become this big-wave mystique.

CHAPTER 2

The Pioneers

The ride was about a mile and an eighth. Yeah, about
a mile and one eighth, and that's a long stretch.

The Duke

The Duke is gone now. But of all the surfers he was Number One, the man who gave surfing stature. He was famous, respected, and loved by everyone who knew him. The Duke gave board riders everywhere a fierce pride in their wild and wet sport. He was also the first really to ride big waves.

Duke didn't talk much about his accomplishments unless asked. His famous mile-and-an-eighth slide would be recalled only when some young surfer sincerely asked, "Duke, what was your longest ride?" Then he would tell what happened long ago at Waikiki, fifty years before the current rage of big-wave surfing. It happened during the era of long boards when surfing was being reborn after a long sleep. It was 1917. A destructive earthquake had just destroyed much of Japan, and swells generated by the *taunami* ranged far across the Pacific. These quake-swells brought twenty-five foot surf—Castles Surf—and Duke and his friend Dad Center paddled out after those swells—nobody else wanted to try.

Duke Paoa Kahanamoku's life was filled again and again with experiences that made him a legend—a heroic figure long before he died early in 1968. The Duke started surfing back in the days when the surfer population of Hawaii

numbered only five or six. A pure Hawaiian, he had a remarkable athletic career that took him swimming and surfing around the world—to three Olympic Games and to top
place in any swimming and surfing hall of fame.

Duke's name came not from his royal Hawaiian lineage
but from his father, who was named in honor of Alfred
Ernest Albert, then the Duke of Edinburgh. Duke was
given Albert's title as part of his father's name. The middle
name, Paoa, is pure Hawaiian. Duke was born in 1890, one
of five brothers. The family grew up around Waikiki, then
unspoiled and unravaged by real estate developers. He
began surfing at the age of four.

Duke was a natural in the water and on a board. He was
already twenty-one—almost over-the-hill by today's competitive standards—when he first splashed into the swimming world, as a contestant in the first Hawaiian AAU meet
back in 1911. He chose the 100-meter free style event.
Duke won the race, but something was wrong at the
judges' stand. The officials were all arguing over their stop
watches. When the poolside debate ended, Duke was told
he had just broken the world's record—by 4.6 seconds.
The next year Duke went on to win his first Olympic gold
medal.

The Duke set his first Olympic free style record in the
1912 Stockholm games. He bettered this time and again
set a new world's record at Antwerp in 1920, only to aston-
ish swimmers by bettering his record once more at the
Paris Olympics in 1924. There was another swimmer at
Paris, though, who had a faster time—Johnny Weissmuller.
At the Los Angeles Olympics, the Duke, at forty-two, just
hadn't the speed to swim sprints—he had to settle for the
Captain's spot on Hawaii's great water polo team.

When Duke wasn't swimming, he was surfing. Between
the 1912 and 1920 Olympics, he and his brother, Dan,
went on a world-wide tour to demonstrate their remarkable
ability in the water. One stop on the tour was Australia.
The Duke took a close look at the waves off Sydney's
Freshwater Beach and decided it was time the Aussies took
up surfing.

There had been a few old-time surfboards in Australia
prior to the Duke's arrival, but nobody had come along to

Haleiwe Bay on Oahu's North Shore, where the crowds are thick.

(P. L. Dixon)

show the locals how to use suitable boards. One Australian had imported a long twelve-footer from Hawaii but, unable to master the art, had turned the plank into a giant ironing board. What the Australians needed was an example to follow; Duke was the perfect master to imitate.

The Duke and his brother went to a local lumber yard, selected the materials, and chipped out what they considered the best design for Australian surf conditions. The Duke launched the long board and put on a surfing display that old-timers around Sydney still remember.

The Duke's example was all the Australians needed, and in the years since, surfing has become the number one seaside sport there. Today, most of Australia's vast beaches have been explored and surfed—and the whole island continent has become a wave-surrounded surfer's paradise.

The Duke also gave surfing another facet: tandem riding. It was in 1910 that the Duke took a woman partner to sea on his long board. Together they began tandem surfing, giving a start to the aquatic acrobatics which are now part of every major surfing competition. Duke then sailed across the Tasman Sea to New Zealand and rode his board off Wellington Beach, another surfing first.

Young surfers from Hawaii still pass along the story of Duke's longest ride, in 1917. The huge swells generated by the Japanese earthquake arrived off Waikiki with the dawn of a cloudless tropical day. Out at sea twenty-five footers pounded over the coral reefs—larger than anyone could remember having seen before, or since.

Duke and his friend, Dad Center, were up at sunrise and out on the water waiting for the heavies. The Duke recalled that they were so far out to sea that they were able to recognize and wave to the captain of a passing steamer. Duke also recalled that the sea was smooth, almost glasslike, and the swells so far apart that there was time to paddle out between sets. When the huge swells came, Dad Center took off on the first of the set. Duke waited for the next and larger wave. It came, towering and about to crash on him. Duke paddled, began his slide down the wave face, and then came to his feet for the ride of his life. He pulled out of the wave a mile and an eighth closer to shore.

One of the last photos of The Duke. Here with Fred Van Dyke,
Butch Van Artsdalen, and Diamond Head in the background. (P. L. Dixon)

He had caught what was probably the longest ride ever experienced by a surfer at that time.

Surfers all over the world respected the Duke. He was never washed-up, over-the-hill, or beyond his prime. And nobody among the surfers called him Mister; it was always "Duke," but always said with respect and some awe. If anyone was ever King of the Surf, it was the Duke. He made frequent appearances at surfing contests and as late as December 1967 was on hand to watch the contest named after him. As Duke watched the big-wave action off Sunset Beach, he would recall that he had surfed there once on his old sixteen-footer, but most of the time he and a few close friends would *bodysurf* Waimea and Sunset, and that was long before swimming fins were added to help start the slide on the big ones.

When not in the water, Duke found time to be elected sheriff of Honolulu, thirteen times in a row; he was the city's ambassador and official greeter. He also appeared in many Hollywood movies, from the twenties right up to the late sixties. The surfers gave him honor after honor, all deserved. In the age of put-down, Duke was always respected for his presence, and not for his past glories alone. When introduced at the 1966 Huntington Beach U.S. Surfing Championships, he was given a five-minute standing ovation, in contrast to the catcalls and laughter that greeted other celebrities.

Today the Duke has gone, but he will forever stand as a symbol of Hawaii, the surf, and all that is good and clean about sports and competition. The white-haired and tough old Hawaiian had given the Islands and surfing more dignity and respect than all the travel posters or hula girls ever assembled by a tourist agency. People who met the Duke or had a chance to hear him speak always remember his greeting or parting—his "Aloha." When it came with Duke's deep-voiced sincerity, it was never forgotten.

The Duke didn't surf alone, nor was he the first. There were others. As far back as the eleventh century, so archeologists say, the islanders of Oceania, across the far Pacific, were surfers, as were New Zealand's Maoris. When Polynesians from Tahiti and Bora Bora landed among the

Hawaiian Islands, they brought their ceremonial surf-boards. One still stands in Honolulu's Bishop Museum.

And when Captain Cook dropped anchor off the big island of Hawaii in 1778, he witnessed surfing and recorded the remarkable sight in his ship's log: "The boldness and address, with which we saw them perform their difficult and dangerous maneuvers (surfing) was altogether astonishing and is scarce to be credited!" Cook's log also mentions canoe and women surfers.

The missionaries who arrived in Hawaii in the early 1800's said surfing was ungodly and should be banned along with gambling, scanty clothing, and sexual freedom. And the Hawaiians suffered greatly learning the Christian ways. Cultural shock and disease reduced the native population from about a half-million to fifty thousand by the late 1880's.

Then came a few sporting types from the mainland United States who gathered at Waikiki with Hawaiians like Duke and again took up the old Hawaiian boards. Jack London described his wet experience in "A Royal Sport," a chapter in his *The Cruise of the Shark*. The crude vigor of London's writing makes this 1900 account more than an historical oddity. He conveys with great strength the thrill of surfing. Soon, surf clubs were organized and surfing photographs were featured in tourist booklets enticing visitors to romantic Hawaii. By 1910, *Haoles* and Islanders were riding the spilling breaks off Waikiki's inside break. Only a very few dared even look to the far, outer horizon where the heavies, the "bluebirds and the smokers" broke big and white a mile and more from the gentle beach-break where the huge hotels now stand.

During this era the boards were short and thin and not really shaped well for big-surf sliding. Lorrin Thurston, with an eye to the big outside waves, developed a twelve-foot board. Soon he and Duke and Dad Center were on their way out to the horizon for Waikiki's Castle Surf. The long board period had begun and the boards grew and grew until some of the old-timers were surfing fifteen-footers made of a good hundred and fifty pounds of redwood.

Meanwhile, back across the Pacific along the California

coast, the developers of the now-vanished Pacific Electric Railway were having a mild depression. They needed some gimmick to lure paying passengers out to Redondo Beach. Most of the traffic was then headed inland to the then-deserted San Fernando Valley. Rabbit hunting from street-cars was so good in the Valley that not many people were visiting the beaches. The management of harassed Pacific Electric found their passenger lure in George Freeth, an Irish-Hawaiian who back in 1907 could really ride a board. Even then he had learned the art of cutting across a wave to race the break—something the rest of the surfing world didn't master for another thirty years. His surfing show at Redondo Beach did the trick—Californians soon went Hawaiian, and in the next decade surfing became established from the Mexican Border clear north to San Francisco.

George Freeth came close to realizing the potential of wave-riding, but he was limited by the long board and a lack of the current philosophy that says get in there with the break, slide into the tube, get the feel of that monster you're trying to master.

Duke followed Freeth a few years later, rode a wave five hundred yards at Corona del Mar and stoked the locals. He then went to the East Coast, bodysurfed the New York beaches, and sailed for the Olympics. Later, Duke surfed a board at New Jersey's Atlantic City pier—the first man to ride the Atlantic's waves.

So the thirties rolled in, the depression was on, and the people who still had money and time for a South Seas vacation discovered Hawaii, the Lurline, and the pink Royal Hawaiian Hotel. Off Waikiki they rode tandem with the beach boys and sent home funny pictures of themselves, red and peeling, standing next to long, hollow surfboards. Surfing was the thing to do before lunch, or before cock-tails. They would go home, paste the funny picture in the family album, and tell their kids how they had surfed in Hawaii during the old days. It was easy, neat. Yet it was adventure, even when being held on the board by a beach boy. A few got hooked and found surfing more than just "something you must do in Hawaii." These few went beyond Waikiki and found waves that were impossible to ride tandem, impossible to ride without dedication and skill and a desire to find out something about oneself. These were the old-timers who climbed into battered and rusting Model A Fords and found Makaha and the North Shore around Kaeana Point.

Back across the Pacific, along the California beaches, surf conditions didn't favor the dilettante vacationer. The waves didn't come spilling in gently as in Waikiki—and the water was colder; so cold that only the young and dedicated wanted to paddle out. There were plenty of these young men, just waiting for a chance to ride the waves. And in the thirties a few of the pioneers at places like San Onofre, Corona del Mar and Paddleboard Cove started sliding really good-sized surf. Old Doc Ball, now living away from the ocean in the mountains, snapped the first really dramatic surfing pictures. They appeared in Sunday supplements and even in the *Saturday Evening Post*—a nickel then. And the young men of California were hooked.

The one Californian who really did most to help surfing was Preston "Pete" Peterson—surfing's Iron Man. Through Pete's experiences we can see the whole scope of surfing—from the twenties right on through today, when he recently won the International Surfing Championship tandem event at Makaha.

CHAPTER 3

Surfing's Iron Man

The surf was so big I cleared the end of Malibu Pier by 100 yards. That was '36.

Pete Peterson

Pete Peterson can sit and spin stories hour after hour about his forty-eight years of surfing, swimming, movie-stunt work and commercial diving and fishing. Pete has won more surfing and paddling and swimming events than any other man alive—and he's not talking about the distant past alone. In 1966, after entering the Makaha International Surfing Championships five times, Pete finally took first place in the tandem event with his pretty, petite partner Barry Algaw—at age fifty-five. He and Barry have also won the last twelve tandem surfing events they had entered.

Pete's a big man, just slightly balding and only a few pounds heavier than when he and Lorren Harrison first sailed to Hawaii back in 1932. They left California to surf the then-uncrowded waves between Waikiki and Honolulu. With them were their self-made surfboards, hollow wooden twelve-footers that didn't weigh much more than today's foam and glass models.

Pete remembers being in the water paddling and surfing between Waikiki and Honolulu a good forty hours a week. Almost all of the Hawaiian surfing in those days took place off Waikiki where the giant hotels now stand.

Most of the surfers of the late twenties and early thirties were a bit introverted. They would simply paddle out, find

Pete Peterson and Barry Algaw on their way to winning the 1966 Makaha
International Surfing Championships tandem event. (P. L. Dixon)

a break, and surf until they were too tired to ride any-more. Pete used to enjoy taking off at dawn, paddling out to Waikiki for a few rides, then cruising up and down the reef surfing spots that looked promising. His daily surf trips involved a good eight miles of paddling, plus working back out to the break after a ride in.

Pete's first visit to the North Shore was a walking- and hitch-hiking trip around Oahu. It was quite an excursion in those times and required three days. He and Lorren Harrison were following the tracks of the old, now-gone Oahu Railroad. They passed by what Pete says is the now famous Pipeline. The two men were intrigued by the awe-some power of the fast-cracking waves. Both were life-guards and wondered if they could survive a swim in the powerful surf. Since there wasn't a single person along that portion of the North Shore, they went out nude—the first surfers to visit the Pipeline went skinny-dipping.

Pete remembers that a big surf was running and that they really felt the power of the Pipeline. It was too big to use their boards so they just swam in and out among the waves to test themselves and the surf's force.

Surfing didn't move out from Waikiki until after World War II. First, Makaha was popular; then the exodus to the North Shore began. Pete was in the first Makaha Contest with Ruth Lee and came second behind Walt Hoffman and his partner. He has returned to Hawaii winter after winter, sometimes surfing tandem for fun and sometimes in contests.

Pete is the present king of the small group of tandem surfers who regularly perform at all large surfing meets. Pete picked up his first lessons in riding double from the Hawaiians. He remembers watching the Duke ride with a pretty young girl and thinking it would be great to take a girl out. "Sometimes when the surf's slow it gets kind of dull riding alone."

Today's tandem team, Pete feels, has to be half acrobat and half skilled surfer. The girl partner should be acro-batically inclined, trained in ballet—and not much over a hundred pounds. Pete gives much of the credit for his many wins to his partners. "I think the girl is the most important half of the team. No matter how well you surf and do the lift, if the girl looks like a sack of flour up there you won't get many points."

Barry Algaw, who has won many contests with Pete, has been his best partner. "Barry's real good. She works hard. Only trouble is she can't swim worth beans. In big surf I worry about her." When it's big, Barry has to sit on the beach—Pete has surfed tandem at Sunset on fifteen- and sixteen-foot days. "Only a girl that's got guts and can swim well should go out there."

Pete feels that a good smooth point break such as Sunset or Makaha is best for tandem because when the board is on a good angle you can forget surfing and concentrate on the lifts. Because of the popularity of tandem-surfing events at the contests, more and more of the younger surfers are finding partners and entering. Pete has led the way and the others are following.

Pete saw his first surfboard resting on the sand in front of his dad's bathhouse on Santa Monica Beach. Pete was seven then and he and his family had just moved from Texas. Pete's folks had been in the hotel business in Kingsville, Texas. Times were hard and they sold out, moved to Santa Monica, and opened a bathhouse.

The first Hawaiians to visit California used to come to Pete's parents' bathhouse to surf and swim—and Pete used to let the Islanders in free in return for the use of their boards. This was back in 1920 when the first planks arriving in California came from Hawaii—built with California redwood.

Pete has lived around Santa Monica all his life and knows the California surf better than anyone. He still surfs the remote offshore channel islands and quietly drives to isolated secret spots he keeps to himself, and down to San Onofre when the surf's up.

Pete designed and built the first balsa boards used in California. He feels strongly about a misconception that has crept into surfing history. Here's how he explains it:

"There's one error I'd like to bring out. Some of the fellows who are supposed to be old-timers talk and write about the heavy redwood boards they were riding back in the thirties. They make it seem like we all lugged around those hundred-pounders. Well gosh, that just wasn't so. A couple of guys from Florida, in the early thirties, built the first balsas and shipped them to Hawaii . . . and they were really keen.

"And when I came back after trying them I started building balsa boards . . . this was in '33. The top surfers back then were riding ten-foot balsa boards that weighed under twenty pounds. They were that light because we didn't have fiberglass to cover them with. Later on we added redwood noses and tailblocks for strength and that brought the weight up."

Paddleboards were very popular then both for surfing and racing. Paddling races attracted large crowds and there were contests almost every week during the summer. Building paddleboards was a common project in high school wood shops around Southern California, and many hundreds were hand-constructed before World War II. Most of the surfers of the late thirties and early forties learned on school-built hollow paddleboards.

The first thirty-five-mile mainland-to-Catalina Island paddleboard race was between Tom Blake, Wally Burton, and Pete. At first the three had just planned a paddling excursion, something to do for a day, but the publicity men from Santa Monica got hold of the story and turned it into a race between "California's Three Top Watermen." Pete recalls that Wally became seasick shortly before they reached the Island. He hung back to help Wally while Tom, by mutual agreement, went on to win the race. Later, when paddleboard clubs grew bigger, ten-man relays were held between Santa Monica and Catalina; paddleboard water-polo clubs started, and paddleboards, sometimes called "kook boxes," replaced the solid wooden boards as surfers' favorites. These were exciting days for water sports in California, but World War II took most of the men away and it wasn't until the late forties that the Golden State again became the leader in aquatics.

Pete is at his best in big surf. He is confident, careful, and one of the best judges of how a wave will react. Surprisingly, in all Pete's years of surfing he remembers that the best and biggest waves to hit California came rolling in just ten years ago, during the summer of 1958. Here is how he described the unusually heavy waves that slammed into Southern California beaches during the 4th of July holidays:

"We've had some really big surf run off California, but the best hit just about ten years ago, the summer my daughter Lisa was born. The surf was so huge it was breaking outside of the tankers moored below Santa Monica. Golly! It must have been cracking a good three-quarters of a mile out . . . and the tug boats behind the Santa Monica Harbor breakwater had to wait for a lull between sets of waves before they could make it out to sea. There weren't too many surfing then so none of the spots really got crowded. Anyway the guys were going crazy, running up and down the coast looking for the best spots. We found the best break right at home, at Sunset Boulevard. It was so big that only two of us made it out there."

Elsewhere along California's coast, the lifeguards were having a horrible time. On the Los Angeles City beaches, the guards made over three hundred rescues on the 4th and 5th of July. At Zuma Beach, north Malibu, the waves were so rough that the victims couldn't be brought to shore through the rips. They had to be taken to a pier by the rescue boat.

One surfer on a mat went out at Point Dume and got a ride of over a mile. Old-timers like Joe Quigg and Mat Kivlin are said to have been so stoked, and spent so much time rushing around, that they never did get in the water. Malibu's waves were a consistent ten feet for three days and the surf was so fast only the very best could handle it.

It was killer surf. The only Negro surfer riding back tried to make a wave across the far end of Malibu Pier and hit the pilings. Pete was on the wave behind him and pulled out before reaching the pier. He swam in among the pilings after the surfer but it was too late. The barnacle-covered pilings had done their work. That accident stopped the attempts to ride beyond the pier's end.

The only other really outstanding super-surf day that Pete recalls was during the summer of 1936—the best day he ever saw at Malibu. There were only a few who rode Malibu then. Pete remembered that he had to call his surfing friends and plead with them to make the long drive up to Malibu and surf with him. "We had a lot of big surf the summer of '36. One outstanding wave started to build far outside the point. I was lucky to be in a good position. It came and I got it. It held and held and the shoulder was peeling off perfectly. I held a good angle and made it beyond the end of the pier by a good hundred yards."

During the early thirties, Pete's friend, Willy Grigsbe, was one of the first to surf Malibu. Willy brought the others along so he wouldn't have to surf alone. In those days the whole cove was fenced off and a wooden walk followed the shore. Willy and some of the others formed the Pacific Coast Surfing Association. Mrs. Adamson, who owned the land which has since become Surfrider Beach, cooperated with the Association and gave the members keys to enter her land and reach the water. Pete claims that no cowboys ever shot at the surfers, nor did Mrs. Adamson ever chase them away.

Two of the more famous-around-the-beach Pete Peterson stories involve his use of kelp seaweed and wax—the seaweed to make the board slick, the wax *on the bottoms of his feet*. Pete says there's absolutely no truth to the tale that he rubbed the top of his board with seaweed to make it slick. But Pete likes to move around a lot on the board and he would sometimes rub wax on the bottoms of his feet instead of on the top deck of the board.

Another—and wholly true—story points to Pete's resourcefulness at sea. Several years ago, Pete had a very fast Jeffries twenty-four-footer, a plywood-hulled and fiberglass-covered powerboat, the *Mike*. Pete used the *Mike* for diving trips, commercial fishing, and for jaunts to surf Southern California's offshore islands. On a voyage out to Santa Barbara Island for sea bass, the *Mike* struck a large floating object hidden just underwater.

It was several hours before dawn and the sea was clothed in a dense fog. Pete felt the hull strike the object. The boat shuddered from the impact and immediately slowed as the bilge began to fill with water.

"We were fourteen miles out, and a long way from the usual ship lanes and probably not another boat within twenty miles. I had to look in the bilge to see where the water was coming in, and there was our bait tank sitting atop the hatch. It was full of water and must have weighed five hundred pounds. It's funny what you can do when your life depends on it. Anyway, my partner and I grabbed that tank and had it over the side in seconds."

When he looked below and saw the water gushing in, Pete grabbed a hand ax, chopped a hole in the stern, and then ran for the throttle. He jammed it forward. The motor surged and as the *Mike* got under way, the bow lifted and the water in the bilge poured out through the hole Pete had chopped in the stern.

Pete knew that if the *Mike*'s motor quit, they'd go down like a stone. "That far offshore we wouldn't have a chance. Putting on the life jackets would only prolong the agony. I tell you we really listened to every little noise that engine made."

The boat kept running. At first Pete thought of heading straight for the nearest land and letting the boat sink off the beach, but it isn't in Pete's nature to give up. He double-checked his course and then turned the boat toward Santa Monica. They arrived back at the pier just after dawn, but there wasn't anyone about to help them. Pete then made a high-speed pass off the end of the pier and tooted the harbor master awake. On the second pass he yelled for the man to have the boat hoist and slings ready.

When the slings were in the water and waiting, Pete brought the *Mike* up in a fast dash and shot between the waiting cables. He cut the motor and the boat sank immediately, but the *Mike* rested on the slings and Pete and his boat were raised high and dry to the safety of the pier. Another example of a resourceful man thinking his way to overcome the sea.

The *Mike* and Pete were involved in another incident that same summer—and again fourteen miles out to sea from Santa Monica. "Everything seems to happen out there in the deep blue." That was the distance offshore where the sport fishing boat *Spare Time* blew apart with a shattering roar. Thirteen people were aboard.

The *Spare Time* was a thirty-three-footer owned and skippered by Wes Wiggins. Wes had built her carefully and lovingly with his own hands and was one of the most conscientious of skippers and "a fanatic on safety." The *Spare Time* had cast off from Santa Monica in the early hours of a clear July morning, headed for Catalina Island and a day's fishing. Early in the afternoon, after cooking lunch on the boat's two-burner butane stove, Skipper Wiggins turned the *Spare Time* about and headed back for Santa Monica.

In the galley a copper line delivering gas to the stove had somehow split, or worked loose, and the heavier-than-air butane gas had filled the bilges. On deck was a bait tank with an electric pump which circulated water to keep the anchovies oxygenated and alive. The pump was located in the bilge. Someone turned on the pump. As the current reached the motor, a tiny spark jumped from the electric line to the armature and—caroom! The blast tore apart the *Spare Time*.

Two men inside the cabin died instantly. Those on deck were hurled through the air to land amidst the shattered wreckage of the boat—fourteen miles from land. Soon the sharks—sleek pelagic blues—arrived, attracted by blood from the injured, and by the day's catch which floated among the men.

Night came. On Santa Monica Pier, Pete Peterson, then a lifeguard lieutenant, was holding down the night shift. Pete was growing worried about the *Spare Time*. She was long overdue. The wives and families of the passengers and crew had gathered to await word on the boat. From years of experience on the sea, Pete knew that most boats are usually overdue because of engine failure, or because they have moored somewhere to escape bad weather.

Pete also knew that the weather was fine and that Wiggins' boat was so well maintained that mechanical trouble was unlikely. He looked into the night, then at the faces of those waiting in the darkness, and grew increasingly worried. Pete had already reported the *Spare Time* overdue, and the Coast Guard and other rescue agencies would start to search at dawn. But dawn was still hours away.

In the water, clinging to bits of shattered wreckage, the survivors, who now numbered five, shook and shivered from their long exposure in the cold water. Mr. Harold

Haley recalled: "The sharks were still filling the black water with eerie streaks of phosphorescence." The survivors could see the lights of Los Angeles twinkling in the distance. The night was "remarkably clear" and fishing boats out of Malibu were seen following the shore. One of the remaining five went mad and began grinning and cackling aloud. He ripped off his clothes and beat at the sharks. Completely nude and raving, the man died and slipped underwater.

As dawn approached, a fog began to drift in toward Santa Monica. As first light began to punch through the haze, Pete set off in the *Mike* with his fourteen-year-old son. "I headed straight out. I had a hunch the *Spare Time* would be directly off Santa Monica.

"The *Mike* was a fast little boat. She could do thirty knots, the fastest boat in Santa Monica. I eased her out of the breakwater and let her run as fast as the fog would permit.

"I began to find wreckage fourteen miles out, three or four little chunks of wood at first. The next recognizable thing I saw was the skipper's chair, which I'd sat on when towing the *Mike* home a couple of weeks before. As soon as I saw that, I knew the boat had blown up. I turned and ran upwind and up current until I found more wreckage. There were plenty of sharks, and they were exceptionally active—more than I've ever seen out there. Every little piece of wreckage was being nudged by them or had toothmarks on it."

Because of Pete's knowledge of local currents and winds, he had found the area of the accident quickly. The other rescue groups were miles away and searching uselessly in the wrong direction. Pete returned to Santa Monica (he had no radio aboard), broadcast the heading from the pier, gassed up, and set out again. He picked up a friend, Ray Heath, because "Ray had the best darn eyesight of any man I've ever known."

Shortly after Pete left Santa Monica for the second time, the fog began to lift and Pete opened the *Mike* up. Overhead were aircraft and helicopters, and on the water every fishing boat Pete had organized for the search.

"I started searching at the small wreckage. I ran a square

area, five minutes one way, five the other. At about 9:30 I came on the first castaways. I almost missed them, but Ray Heath saw something quite aways off. I thought it was a pelican, but we ran over to investigate—and found two men clinging to a long flat board surrounded by sharks." Pete picked them up and continued the hunt for the others, finding the last man shortly thereafter. The three men he saved were the only ones found.

The lifejackets of the missing were found, all with sharks' toothmarks on them. One body was recovered, completely gutted by sharks. One man who knew what he was doing had accomplished more than the combined air-and-water hunt of dozens of aircraft and hundreds of boats. That's the kind of canny and quiet determination typical of Pete.

Pete has also had his share of underwater adventures on movie stunt jobs. Since the 1930's, he has been one of the top Hollywood water-stunt men. In the movie business the stunt guys have their specialties. There are horse men, car men, fight men, high-work men, and water men. Pete sometimes works fights and drives stunt cars but water work has been his specialty and he has earned a very good reputation at it.

You'll see Pete in most of the old South Seas adventures, in many of the *Sea Hunt* episodes—playing an "enemy diver"—and inside almost all the monsters in *Voyage to the Bottom of the Sea*. In fact Pete is one of the very few water men who can stand the very dangerous and confined restrictions of an underwater-monster costume. He's had his share of close calls, moments down below when he was completely blinded and weighted down by hundreds of pounds of soggy foam-rubber costume.

"By far the most miserable thing I've ever done is work underwater in those darn costumes. To start with you're in that foam rubber, completely buttoned up helpless, and the claws are fixed on so you couldn't help yourself if you had to. You're completely dependent on your safety man. And you can't see a thing. I don't know of any water man who's worked in monster suits who hasn't nearly drowned . . . I tell you I've really suffered in those darn things."

What does surfing do to a man after forty-eight years of being in the water almost every day? What are the effects, physically and mentally? Pete may be unique, not the right person to use as an example, but he's the only man available who has devoted that great a span of life to surfing and water sports.

Pete stands tall. His posture, his wide back and knotted arms, show his great strength. His back and chest muscles are smooth and long, the mark of a competitive swimmer. He's a bit heavier than in the thirties when he starred in seven Pete Smith movie shorts. These were popular short subjects for which Pete surfed, water-skied, and made underwater movies.

The only observable effect of his long exposure to sun, sand, and sea water is a slight sensitivity to sun. Pete usually wears a hat when working around the water, and when he's surfing for long periods in Hawaii he'll wear a T-shirt to cut the strong ultra-violet rays. Pete's still the Iron Man, still surfing, paddling, and swimming long distances with graceful ease.

During the winter of 1967–68, Pete suffered a slight accident while surfing tandem. He was off surfing for awhile, resting a twisted neck and sore shoulder. While resting, he worked on his Hawaiian beach house right below the Pipeline where he swam so many years ago during his first visit to the North Shore. A young surfer dropped by to visit him. The day was hot and Pete suggested a swim. As they left the house for the surf, Pete grabbed a diving mask.

The visitor followed Pete through the crashing shore-break and was amazed at the ease he showed working through the dumping waves. They gained the relatively calm water beyond the surfline. Even with his stiff shoulder, Pete set a fast pace for deeper water. He stopped over the outside reef, thirty-five feet below. He put on the mask and dove down, effortlessly and without fins, right to the bottom.

Pete proceeded to swim along the coral, inspecting caves and possible hiding places of the elusive Hawaiian lobster.

Up above, the young surfer, also an excellent diver, waited and worried. At last Pete came up, handed him the mask, took a couple of deep breaths, and swam on. The youngster knew it was his turn. He put on the mask and dove. He made it to the bottom, but could stay only long enough to turn around and hurtle back to the surface. Just a brief example of the Iron Man's remarkable stamina and ability both on and under the water.

And what about Pete's thoughts, his philosophy, his mind that figures quietly and then carries his thoughts into action? Pete today is a relaxed and successful man. He divides his time between his business of installing moorings for the many boats around Los Angeles, building his own designed rescue tubes for lifeguard services all over the world, and a variety of jobs calling for his special talents.

Pete hates sloppy jobs and takes pride in doing careful work on any task he attempts. The many boats and boards he has built over the years show his attention to detail of workmanship. He also likes to innovate, to dream up new ways of doing old jobs better. For a promoter he designed a pair of water skis for an elephant, taught the pachyderm to mount the skis, and then took the two-ton animal for a ski around Santa Monica Harbor.

His home in fashionable Sullivan Canyon in the Santa Monica Mountains shows the balance Pete and his wife Alice maintain between the life of surfing and water work, and a normal dry-land environment. Pete's office, however, contains the mementoes and treasures of his active life, plus the tools of his trade, favorite old surfboards he'd never sell and the odds and ends of half a dozen projects he's always working on.

Surfing—that's still Pete's big thing in life. He may give up tandem riding and contests in years to come, but he'll never give up riding waves. "I figure a man can keep riding as long as he can paddle out to the break. Look at 'Pop' Proctor. He's eighty-three and still surfing. I know I'll beat him by at least ten years."

Pete's neither young nor old, he's just himself—tough, dependable, able to move on, around, and under water better than almost any man alive.

CHAPTER 4

Malibu—The Special Wave

Malibu was like an endless party of excitement. Each
day offered something else, something new and special.

John Fain

Summer, 1968. A skinny kid from Brooklyn steps off a
silver jet. He threads his way through the impersonal airport corridors to find the baggage area. He looks anxiously
for his surfboard. It comes down the conveyer belt, gleam-
ing red and white among the leather and plastic cases. He
checks it—no cracks or fractures. With a canvas TWA bag
in one hand and his board under the other arm he leaves
the airport, curls his tongue behind his teeth and whistles
up a taxi. "Take me to Malibu, where the surfers are!"

His dream comes true. He has three weeks of freedom
left before the Army takes him and shaves his long hair,
before his pilgrimage to Malibu must come to an end.

He arrives at that special place. The hot sun makes
his acne glare, his eyes blink. It's there: the waves, the
surfers, the girls with their almost nude brown bodies and
long blonde hair. The skinny kid has come a long way from
his teeming New York, his journey a surfer's dream come
true. This young man and thousands more have come
because of Malibu's special appeal, a unique flavor found
nowhere else in the surfer's world. Though the original
Malibu surfing crowd has gone, two facets have remained
constant—the wonderful waves and the glamour to be
found along this short stretch of beach.

35

The waves of Malibu are as special as the people because they arrive as near to perfect as nature can make them. The people, the kids with surfer "bumps," the newly arrived, all come with a compelling desire to savor the full-course day of delights that is uniquely Malibu. Here's the story of Malibu, a story of the characters and the waves—a true story that still continues to unfold, an old story that began when Malibu Indians dug for clams before the Spanish made them Christians and so sick in body and soul that they are no more.

It is not Waikiki, Saint Tropez, or Biarritz. But to young Sou iern Californians, Malibu Beach is special—uniquely their own. On any day when surf from the vast Pacific rolls into the rather small cove called Malibu, the surfers will be there, all fighting for their place on the waves. On the beach will be their blonde, bikini-clad girls, the hippies, the curious from inland America carrying their Kodaks, and a large group of non-surfing males come to watch the surfers' spectacular girls.

Along all of California's varied coastline there's only one Malibu. Malibu, so close to Hollywood, draws its surf- and sand- and sun-loving crowd from a population of almost eight million. The beach couldn't possibly accommodate more than five thousand at one time, but these five thousand and sometimes more represent what is both glorious and ignoble about Southern California. Malibu lies just a few fast freeway-miles north of big, busy Los Angeles. The freeways dump their traffic on the long coastal highway and during summer weekends traffic actually stops for hours at a time. Yet beyond the lines of steaming cars and impatient, frustrated drivers, the waves of Malibu roll steadily shoreward—a beautiful testimony to the truth that nature rises above all the mechanized society that has come to observe her beauty.

Malibu is blessed with an unusual social and geographic setting. The beach itself and the underwater topography beyond have combined to produce a seaside environment which creates some of the finest surfboard-riding waves found anywhere in the world. The waves that roll toward the beach with such mechanical precision aren't the huge combers of Hawaii, but they are perfect for that fast, flashy,

Even on a small-surf day, Malibu's waves peel off the point with
machinelike precision. (Dixon collection)

"hot-dogging" style of surfing typical of Southern California. When a storm from tropic Mexico or South America sends powerful ground swells northward, the waves of Malibu show their best form. This has been so ever since the seas stabilized millenniums ago.

Today the surfers, the beachgoers of Southern California regard Malibu with that same special affection golfers have for their favorite green, that mountaineers have for the difficult yet climbable peaks of the Alps. Most of today's best wave riders learned to surf at Malibu, met their first girl friend there, had their first fight alongside the water's edge, and took their first drink beside the old wire fence that separates the public beach from the private land beyond.

Malibu is where it's all happening, where the whole Southern California scene could be viewed by a foreign visitor with only one day to spend and wanting to see what's "in" and who's doing what.

Along this half mile of beach the one-day visitor could observe all the "kooky," "kickey," and "groovy" happenings so typical of the Southern California beach scene. But he would still miss much of what's really going on. You have to be a part of Malibu, a part of the surfing crowd to get a real insight.

It would be hard to tell who's really the number one surfer in the minds of the sprawling bikini-clad girls. It would be impossible to know that the typical, healthy, "all-American" kid on the red-and-white surfboard has been busted twice by the police on a narcotics charge, or that the lovely eighteen-year-old girl with the long blonde hair and wearing a muu muu is dating a Hollywood movie producer. The kids lying on the sand know all this—but it's part of the scene and they make no judgment; they accept.

Then there are the surfers who just surf. The majority of the Malibu gang don't smoke pot, or drink—they simply surf and enjoy themselves. The majority of the tanned and muscled young men glory in the waves, come alive racing across the walls of crashing wet blue-whiteness.

This experience of challenging a nearly perfect nature-made wave is what draws most to Malibu. This is their last frontier—twenty miles from the eight million who hem them in with rules and smog. The sex, the parties, the soul-searching about existence, the talk of war and peace, the free love and everything else quickly diminishes in importance when the waves begin to build and the telephone system spreads the word—"Surf's up!"

Malibu was just a barren point of land pushing out into the Pacific Ocean when the Spaniards first came to California in the early 1500's. A few Indians used to dig clams at low tide, but that's all that really happened at Malibu until the Spanish land holdings were broken and the City of Los Angeles began its explosive growth in the 1920's.

During this same period a very few young Californians were relearning the ancient Hawaiian sport of surfing. These young men came to realize that the Malibu cove was a special place to surf. They said to hell with the fence and the guards, and pushed their long wooden surfboards through the barbed wire and paddled out to face the waves of Malibu.

Then progress overcame resistance to change. Down went the barbed-wire fence and Malibu received roads and land speculators, and at last the marvelous beach of precision waves was opened to the public—and the surfers. This all happened in the 1940's and the surfers came by the fives and the tens and there was room for all, even on a hot, big-wave Sunday.

Then suddenly it happened. In 1957 a screenwriter penned a little novel called *Gidget*. This was the story of a young girl who joined the surfers at Malibu and suddenly learned all about life—fast. And Gidget, a fictitious beach bunny, became the symbol of the surf-set-to-be. Many surfers hold her creator, Frederick Kohner, responsible for the explosive growth of surfing. Surfboard builders may bless him, but the old-time Malibu crowd saw *Gidget* as the beginning of the end of their happy days on the open waves of Malibu. The publication of *Gidget* was the start of a new era which saw thousands and hundreds of thousands grab lightweight plastic foam and fiberglass surfboards and join the surfing fad.

Shortly after the publication of the book came Gidget movies and a Gidget TV series. Then the New York advertising agencies decided the surfing theme would sell products—and they were right. Soon, surfing commercials were selling (and are still selling) breakfast food, tennis shoes —even carpets. The slick sell, the romance and adventure of surfing captured the young public's imagination and surfing became a big-time sport along most beaches of the United States.

Kids from inland America saw the TV commercials, caught the spirit, and hurried along to Malibu. This all happened eight years ago, in the summer of 1960. Many of the boys who ran away from home to surf are still at Malibu, still surfing, and somehow staying young and finding enjoyment and fulfillment in riding a perfect wave. Some grew tired of the Malibu crowd and went on to surf in Hawaii, where the waves are like moving mountains and each ride a dangerous, watery adventure.

The names of some of the top Malibu riders evoke hero worship from teen-agers on the Atlantic Coast, along the Gulf of Mexico, and even as far away as water-surrounded Australia. Mickey Dora, for example, has been called "Mr. Malibu" and worse for years. And John Fain, as good a surfer, has been trying to outride the thirty-four-year-old Dora for the past ten years, ever since he was fourteen years old.

These two have been surfing and fighting each other at Malibu continually. A big-surf day at Malibu wouldn't be complete without a Dora-Fain battle on a six-foot, fast-breaking wave.

Lance Carson comes up number three in the list of Malibu surfers. Lance is putting on weight, his timing is off, and he's now twenty-five. All the seventeen-year-olds are waiting for him to slip; they want his space as number three in the Malibu pecking order. Dora and Fain will never slip; the younger kids are sure of this and only a few try to outride them. However, the number three spot is open because Lance keeps getting heavier. The young surfers watch his weight carefully and it's not unusual to see a grinning towhead leave a box of sugary, high-calorie cookies beside Lance's towel. And Lance, being a realist, can't resist; he knows it's only a matter of time until fat dominates.

There are dozens of other young and not-so-young men

John Fain, intensely competitive, works over a small Malibu wave.
(P. L. Dixon)

who make the Malibu scene whenever the surf comes up. Some are great surfers who show up only when big waves pound in, scaring away the less experienced surfers. Almost every day some sort of unofficial surfing contest is held at Malibu. Somebody is always trying to outride someone. And the competition is rough, as the Malibu Emergency Hospital physician will testify. Beginning at eight in the morning on any crowded big-surf day, and on until after dark, the good doctor sets and stitches and x-rays the injured—all limping in as painful evidence that surfing at Malibu is not all sweet waves and heroic rides.

Ask anyone who has surfed Malibu, ask any of the bikini girls who have browned their backs and bottoms at Malibu, and they'll tell you, "Malibu, man that's a groovy place. Too crowded for me, but I can't keep away." Ask the local sheriff and he'll tell you, "Ought to close that beach down, more trouble than it's worth." Ask the waves—ask those marvelous blue-green waves that break with such precision —and they won't tell. They just make it all happen.

What happened at this special place of waves gave rise to the whole world-wide surfing scene. Johnny Fain and Mickey Dora were there when it began, they still ride there—Johnny almost every day and Mickey when the surf's breaking the way he likes it.

John Fain had his first slide across a Malibu breaker as another one of those skinny kids drawn to its waves. John was thirteen years old before he surfed Malibu. He had learned at the Colony, a surf spot a mile north of the famous Malibu pier. He had been brought along by the pioneers—like Dale Velzy, Dick Zanuck of 20th Century Fox, and movie star Richard Crenna. The Cole Brothers, Matt Kivlin, and Dave Rochlen were among many others who helped John—and after a year at the Colony, John was ready for Malibu. It was good-time surfing then, no competition, no social scene. Then came the "Malibu Hut."

The Hut was the brain storm of Jerry Hersh and "Tube Steak" (Terry Tracy), and four or five of the old Malibu gang. The wilted palm-branch and driftwood hut just grew. Soon a second hut was erected and the good days and wild times began.

Tube Steak was a relaxed organizer. He staged impromptu volleyball games, paddling and surfing contests, and Malibu's unique cocktail hour. Mickey Dora added his special touch—displays of sky rockets and bursting fire-crackers smuggled in from Mexico. John was the youngest. He surfed Malibu every day after school and the good times impressed him. Johnny was like a little puppy hanging around a group of big dogs. The big dogs don't hurt the youngster until it grows up. Then watch out. As John observed, "I was the youngest, everyone looked out for me, but then I started growing and the big guys started growling. It was good training, because I learned so much about my fellow man. I grew up a lot faster. Malibu was like an endless party of excitement because each day offered something else, something new."

From the very first, Johnny wanted to be the best surfer at Malibu. He was the fastest one out on the water, always trying to catch the most waves in the shortest possible time. He'd sometimes crowd others in the wave and the old surfers would "growl," kick their boards out of the wave, striking the skinny kid across the shins. This was the first time John experienced fear. But off the waves, even in summer, the happy atmosphere continued. People would bring horses down on the beach and race; motor-cycles would roar along the hard sand at low tide from the pier to the point. And the women were always there. The atmosphere then was older, less inhibited, and the Malibu crowd would take advantage of everything the beach had to offer.

Take any Tuesday or Thursday, or any day of the week before *Gidget* and the big boom of 1960, and here's a typical Malibu day in summer, or on any sunny day in winter, when the surf was up or down:

First arrivals built a fire, if cold. If the surf was up, they'd ride until lunch. If the surf was down, they skindived for lobster or abalone which would be used for supper.

After lunch of orange juice and fig bars, they rested and napped, or worked on the hut, or helped carry an old, discarded, overstuffed couch down from the road. They'd surf some more if the wind wasn't blowing, or play a couple of games of volleyball. They checked the girls coming down after school.

If it was hot and there was no surf, they'd take a run to the pier, dive off the end and swim to the point. Others, like Dave Sweet, would build surfboards on the beach and let the wind sweep away the huge pile of balsa chips and shavings.

If the surf held and the wind died and the water surface grew glassy, they'd surf until dark, until arms and backs were too tired to paddle out again.

When evening came, the fires would start up, the guitars would be uncased, the wine bottles held in brown paper bags would be brought out, and from somewhere food would appear.

The whole scene was kept cool, so relaxed and quiet that the Malibu sheriffs didn't bother the gang. Their numbers were small at first, but then more and more girls came down to take in the fun, to enjoy the evening party, the food and the Hawaiian atmosphere. The girls found the beach parties exciting and quite a few began spending nights on the sand or in the huts. A few young girls arrived and their parents became alarmed, and the whole free, easy, swinging affair came to the attention of the police.

As Johnny said, "Nobody was getting hurt or in trouble, but the growing crowds and the people nosing in took the fun away." Then the guys who created the Malibu scene said to hell with it. They saw the end coming and burned the huts—their protest against progress. The old couch was tipped into the surf and the currents took it away. Some moved on. Others stayed and adjusted to the change. After all, the waves were still pounding in and the best surfers would always have the best wave days to themselves. The others couldn't manage Mailibu when the surf was up and breaking big off the outside point.

The huge surf of 1958 marked the high point of the Malibu scene. Every surfer who was around then still remembers those two wonderful weeks of exceedingly heavy surf. Johnny, Mickey, Ricky Grigg, and a handful of others who had Malibu "wired" were the only ones capable of handling the huge break—and they turned on like it was never turned on before. This was the beginning of the hot surfer period and the top dogs of Malibu were soon the talk of Southern California.

The waves were almost too much for John. He'd fight out past the break and position himself with the older guys and wait. The swells would come, bigger and faster than anyone had ever seen before. John would take off with the older men and they would cut in front of him, leaving the tumbling white water for the skinny kid to fight and fall off in. Then came John's day, the day when up forward nose-riding came of age.

The next summer the crowds were beginning to arrive. From San Fernando Valley and inland Southern California came the hundreds determined to make the scene at Malibu. Most of them had boards, but not the years of necessary surfing experience or the competitive spirit needed to fight and scrap and battle for a position on the wave. John had gone through it all. He was ready—tempered and strong now, if only fifteen.

John had one of the first light nose-riding boards and when the first big swell of '59 arrived on a hot June morning, the crowd was there. The waves were large, so large that the newly arrived were content to sit on the beach with the girls. The old Malibu Gang had the point to themselves. Among the older surfers was Johnny, still regarded as the skinny little kid who always got in the way.

The set of the morning came, rising high and lifting the long strands of kelp until the stems were pulled so taut that they broke. Six or seven surfers whipped their boards around and got into position. Johnny was crowded in the middle, the worst possible spot. Those to the far side of the collapsing shoulder could pull away from the break. Those closest could turn toward the beach and ride the white water, avoiding a collision. But John was in no man's land. He remembers hearing an older guy swear and say, "Get that little kid out of here. He's going to mess the whole thing up."

John took off. He knew he had to accelerate to escape the press of boards and make the fast-breaking wave. He ran to the nose, trimmed and took off. John thought, This has got to work. This is it! He dropped low, gaining speed, passed two of the riders, and found himself out in front

of the crowd making the wave. He heard their voices cursing him and as he flew shoreward, he saw the beach sitters
coming to their feet and cheering in admiration. It was the
ride of his life, the big slide that urged Johnny forward.
It was a great ride and a great and fabulous summer—the
last summer when the surfing life was free and easy, the
competition informal, and there wasn't a dime to be made
from board-riding.

Dollars and publicity and "beach-party movies" ended
the day-to-day free-swinging surfing life. Surf movies were
distributed to cinemas large and small across America. It
was considered corruption by the Malibu crew, but elsewhere it was a dream to be sought. The rapidly growing
interest in surfing and the beach life created a swift demand for anything connected with surfing, the commercially-
minded saw how the money could pour in—and they went
to work.

The regulars of Malibu grew discouraged. The crowds
were pushing, always pushing their way among the waves.
When the hut burned, Tube Steak didn't have a place to
sleep. He tried the beach and his car. It wasn't the same.
Tube Steak, Malibu's mayor and cruise director, pulled out
and moved south. He was so disenchanted that he went
into real estate and returned to a more conventional world.

The on-the-beach surfboard builders were driven off—
no business license. The Cole Brothers went to work,
Corny as an artist and Peter as a teacher to continue his
love affair with the big surf in Hawaii. Dave Rochlen
dropped into System Development Corporation as a
scientist before moving on to Hawaii and his "Surf-Line"
clothing empire.

Then came the L.A. County Lifeguard Tower and
Authority. Those who wouldn't be discouraged tried to
organize surfing into maturity.

The first efforts were made by the United States Surfing
Association and by contests. But contests brought crowds,
and contest winners received publicity and offers of free
surfboards if they'd endorse them. Then offers of money
and percentages were made to top surfers, plus expenses
for traveling. The beach movies and filmed commercials
lured a lot of young men to scrap for top position because

Micky Dora rides a fast-breaking San Miguel wave during the
first U.S.–Mexican surfing contest. (P. L. Dixon)

the best surfers made the most money. Thus, competition caused hard feelings to grow among all those jockeying for the financial favors.

In Hawaii, money mattered less. The surf would come up and the few who were there then didn't care if the cameras were grinding or the judges were watching. The battle was man against wave—and those who could, left Malibu for The Islands. Some joined the winter migration and found temporary refuge along the North Shore. A few stayed forever.

The best of the early big-wave riders were all immigrants from Malibu. These were the giants who gained their fame as the first to ride the wild winter waves of north Oahu.

Along California's southern coast, the young kids who had joined the big surf explosion of '59 and '60 were coming of age in the surf. Many dropped out after a few sunburns and disenchantment with beach life. These were the ones who hadn't made it through the initial stages of learning to surf and couldn't contend with the growing crowds. The young surfers who remained had all been tested in the wet initiation rites of wipe-outs and collision-caused bruises. The survivors of the crowded wave battles were veterans at fifteen. They'd made the commitment of effort and would hang on. The very young of this period overcame the normal fear most find during the learning process and went on to become the champions of today. Again Malibu was the playing field, where many practiced and where most learned that the mysteries of life were quite simple.

John Fain was one of those fifteen-year-old Malibu surfers who had grown up rapidly. His initiation was not conventional. There were no school affairs for John, no games or dances or proms—life along the beach was more basic, honest.

Nobody cared for hot rods. It was surf and play and try to find some kind of truth. There was no need for the fumbling, the slow growing up of normal teen-age development. The hut was there, and on the beach and by the hut John's education came quickly and firsthand. John's experience was repeated a hundred times at a dozen other beaches by a hundred different wave hunters.

John felt he was lucky. He gained confidence early and was soon one of the top competitive and commercial surfers in California. Surfing was so important for John that he approached it like a pro. He kept away from tobacco, trained, and limited his drinking to a beer or a glass of cold white wine. Contests bring recognition and recognition becomes necessary in the ranks of the pro; from these ranks come the champions who receive the free trips to Peru, Hawaii, Australia and other places where jet tickets run into the hundreds of dollars.

Those on top of the wave get by comfortably. There are the expenses, free board, parts in movies and commercials, endorsement of products, modeling fees. John, for example, has appeared (surfing) in all the beach-party movies, has been very active in TV commercials, and rides for the Jacobs Surfing Team. In one movie John and two other surfers had to make a three-man transfer on a wave. The director thought it would be keen if all three surfers could take off on the same wave simultaneously and end the ride on the same board. Fifteen waves and two hours later they did it. For this type of work the movies pay well.

Another job that came to John-of-Malibu was an assignment to surf with a Playboy Bunnie-of-the-month. Though John was cut out of the gate-fold center spread, he did have two days of very enjoyable surfing—or as he says, "Surfing's fringe benefits."

Malibu doesn't have wave all year round. In winter, when the California water grows cold and the swell direction changes, Malibu sleeps. The best waves come during summer, driven in by South Swells. But in Hawaii, the winter North Swell awakes as the break at Malibu gently laps over the rocks and tide pools and the few surfers who wait patiently in the chill for that chance wave. In winter, the migration from Los Angeles International Airport to Honolulu begins. The first pack up to leave in late October, hoping to catch the first swell to arrive at Waimea or Sunset. By Thanksgiving, all those not in school or working have paid their board-transport charge and are living along the North Shore. The biggest group comes over during Christmas vacation for the contests and the warmth of tropic sun and water.

John Fain has made the winter migration from Malibu to Hawaii three times, staying as long as his budget allows, surfing hard until he's worn out or something breaks. But when the winter big-surf season comes to an end and the North Shore sleeps, John returns to his Malibu. John has made several surfaris to places like Mexico, Puerto Rico, and Peru. He was also the first to take surfboards to Barbados, British West Indies. John, Phil Wilson, and Butch Linden found excellent surf at a spot called Beau Bells. John described the waves as "thin, well shaped like Hawaii's Ala Moana, but with the power of the Banzai Pipeline."

In Peru, John found big surf, but the rugged coastline and the frequently foggy days made the waves seem more forbidding and dangerous. The rocky boulder-strewn shore made wipe-outs shattering experiences. John enjoyed his stay and the difference in waves and people, but summer was coming and the break was starting at Malibu. He had to return because Malibu is John's special place.

Malibu today, in the summer of 1968, has grown more and more crowded. The huge numbers of surfers jammed into the cove make wave-riding both difficult and dangerous. And the battleground of Malibu favors the aggressive, the young kid who's out to make his name, his reputation on the best and wildest surfing spot in Southern California.

John is frequently the target of the up-and-coming young surfers. The young ones know that if they can cut out John, outride and outshine him, their reputations will be enhanced immensely. When John surfs Malibu on a big, fast day, the tension builds because he knows that chances are good some young hot-shot is going to challenge him. It usually happens when John comes ripping along as close to the curling shoulder of the wave as possible. In his critical position there's only room for one. Suddenly he sees another surfer taking off in front of him, so close that a collision is almost impossible to avoid. John knows the guy has jumped in front of him deliberately.

John has two choices: pull out and let the wave hog have it, or fight for his position. John always fights when the wave hog drops in front deliberately. He rises to the top of the wave and passes over the trespasser and warns

him. "OK," says John, "watch it." If the surfer takes warn-
ing and watches the close take-offs, nothing happens. If
not, John is forced to deal with him. And this means that
John has to repeat his action, surf in front of the rider, and
then suddenly cut back to clip him on the leg or shoulder
with his own board. Usually, this works. If it doesn't, the
battle gets hotter, sometimes carrying from the water to
the beach. That's Malibu.

"There was something I'll never forget about the beginning of the Malibu surf scene," John recalls. "It was great.
You'd sit on the beach with your friends and out on the
water would be a beautiful golden bright flash cutting
across those lovely, perfect waves. You'd watch it, watch
the way that speck of color and surfboard would blend as
one with the wave. Then the flash would get tired and
come in to rest and you'd meet a real individual, not a part
of a mob all doing and talking the same thing. That flash
was something to respect, something to try and imitate;
and maybe even after a lot of trying you'd become a flash
of golden brightness yourself.

"That's impossible today. The crowds have dulled
Malibu. You'd never even see that brightness if it happened again. The light would never get past the kooks
crashing their heads together in the shorebreak. Malibu's
dead except for those special days when the surf's so big
only a handful of us can make it out. That's why I still go
back, for those special days. For me it's enough if it happens once a summer. Just maybe I'll get a glimpse of that
wonderful golden color again."

Alas, poor Malibu, dulled and tarnished and covered
with trash and bodies by the thousands and surfboards by
the hundreds, smacking together in endless battles that
produce the surfer's ultimate frustration—perfect waves but
no place left to ride them. Let's leave Malibu. Let's hit the
Islands and the big surf and the dozens of breaks waiting
for the men who ride mountains. Farewell, Malibu.

CHAPTER 5

Coming of Age on the North Shore

I was lost in the channel, and even worse a wave was coming right down at me. The only other thing that I knew of that resembled that huge wall of water was the drive-in movie screen back home.

Fred Van Dyke

Back then, fifteen or so years ago, before Bud Browne's movies and before the first blurry black-and-white photographs hit the mainland, there were just a handful of big-wave riders. They were mainly Islanders, but a few odd and restless Californians had crossed over to surf Hawaii and returned, and slowly the rumors started trickling back to the mainland and up and down the California coast.

The rumors prompted Bob Simmons to check the charts and the archives of the public library and Honolulu's Bishop Museum. Simmons, with his relentless and perceptive ability to find new surf spots, rightly predicted that the North Shore would have the biggest surfable waves in the world. He also discovered among the dusty old texts that the eighth-century prehistory surfers of Hawaii had paddled all the way from Kauai to ride the mountainous surf of the North Shore.

So Simmons charted the spots that later became Sunset Beach of Hawaii, as well as Steamer Lane and Ventura Overhead of California. He also located some of the pre-World War II Hawaiian surfers and learned that Lorren Harrison had brought his bride to Hawaii in the thirties

52

and had taken her tandem-surfing at Haleiwa's outside break—a hair-raising thing to do to a young bride since the reef lies over a half mile from the shore and, when it's breaking, the waves have to be eight- to ten-feet high. Simmons also found out that some of the early body surfers used to slide at the then unnamed spots of Pupukea and Haleiwa.

Simmons, even with his almost useless arm, was able to take his charts and follow them to paddle out and surf the spots he had found through his library research. It seems almost unbelievable now that he was accurate within inches of his predictions. Bob returned to California and his descriptions of the big surf were passed along, and the young men from the States kept talking about going to see for themselves.

One morning, in about the winter of '52, the *Examiner* and others of the Hearst newspaper chain carried a large picture of Makaha surf on the front page. That one photo of Buzzy Trent, George Downing, and Dave Mojas probably lured more of the early surfers to the North Shore than any other single factor. It caught the attention of Fred Van Dyke and was the reason he left the chilling waves of Santa Cruz and a comfortable job as a schoolteacher.

Fred is typical of the early crew that deserted the mainland for Hawaii's surf. Here's how he remembers the day he saw the famous picture. "One morning while I was teaching in that little school up in the Santa Cruz Mountains my superintendent walked into the classroom and showed me the *Examiner*. There was that picture of these three guys standing on what looked like a black mountain. I thought at first they were skiing. Then I thought it must be a fake. I thought again if it's real this idiot superintendent just lost a teacher, and that's when I left for the Islands."

Fred arrived in the Islands to be met by his friend Al Wiemers. They had surfed together at Steamer Lane, Santa Cruz, for many years. Al was stationed at the Marine Corps hospital in Honolulu and surfed every chance he could get. Al took Fred out to Queen's surf off Waikiki and there he met the old-timers of the big surf—Wally Froiseth, Blue Makua, Blackout Whaley and the Duke. He was

impressed with the graceful way they handled the big, outside Queen's break, but it wasn't the surf he had come to
find.

Fred found his guide to the moving mountains of the
North Shore in an ice-cream parlor on Beretania Street,
downtown Honolulu. There, stoking up on a sundae, was
Buzzy Trent. They got to talking about surfing and big
waves and Buzzy looked up at him and said, "Why don't
you ride out to Sunset with me tomorrow? I got a feeling
the surf will be up." Until that time Fred had set a mental,
psychological limit of the size waves he would ride. His
idea of top size for himself was fifteen feet, not really large
for the North Shore.

This was back in '55 and Fred's first meeting with Buzzy,
the man in the newspaper photo he had looked at so often
riding the heavies at Makaha. Fred remembers his first
thoughts after meeting Buzzy:"Wow, this guy is a human
being after all." He had really expected to meet some kind
of a giant, an untouchable Adonis movie-star type. Buzzy,
though strong and ruggedly constructed, wasn't seven feet
tall but just a man who enjoyed ice cream and big surf.
They made an arrangement to meet the next morning.

Fred's surfing buddies warned him that if Buzzy said
he'd meet you at one place at a certain time, the best possible thing to do if you wanted to find Buzzy would be to
go to the most unlikely spot at the most unlikely time and
he'd be there. But Buzzy was where he had promised to be
the next morning and he and Fred set out for Sunset Beach.

As Buzzy's boiling, 1947 wooden station wagon steamed
over the hill just beyond Schofield Barracks, Fred saw the
North Shore for the first time. The windshield was fogged
by steam but far past the cane and pineapple fields the
waves were building, crashing over, and rolling shoreward.
Al Wiemers had come along and both admitted later that
as they looked at the white water showing as far as the
horizon, fear had sliced through their bodies.

Sunset Beach had been "off limits" and "Kapu" for most
surfers because they feared the power of the surf and the
unpredictable way the waves broke. They knew about the
day Mike Stang and Jim Fisher had been caught in the
channel when the whole bay had walled up and crashed

Surf action, early '60s, Sunset Beach, Oahu.
(Photographer unknown, Dixon collection)

over. The wave, which might have been thirty-five feet high, almost drowned them. The white water generated by that tremendous surf washed over the banks and flooded across the highway. And then Buzzy, Al and Fred were at Sunset Beach.

Buzzy took a long look out across the surf and yelled "Come on, you guys, you wanted to ride big waves. Wel: here they are!" The two initiates looked out to sea an watched a giant steep-walled wave crash over from top to bottom. Van Dyke still remembers it: "The wax in my hand felt like it was melting. This wasn't what I had thought it would be like for the first time out."

Buzzy didn't wait for excuses. He unstrapped the boards and changed into his nylon racing suit. He'd had the suit made to order of the lightest possible cloth. Buzzy figured that even six ounces saved on bathing-suit weight would help if he had to swim a long way. Buzzy trotted down the steeply-sloping beach and paddled off. Al followed, but Van Dyke stood and stared bug-eyed at the giant surf.

Then he followed. "In seconds Al and Buzzy disappeared in the wild chop of the shorebreak. Everything was telling me this was out of the question, but I had to do it. The paddle through the rip to the outside line-up wasn't bad. It only took about ten minutes, but I still couldn't find Buzzy or Al. I looked back to shore. It seemed like miles away. Then that panicky feeling started creeping up on me. I was lost in the channel. And even worse, a wave was coming right down at me. The only other thing that I knew of that resembled that huge wall of water was the drive-in movie screen back home in Santa Cruz."

The wave entered deep water and diminished and Fred was able to rise over the top to where he could see Buzzy and Al waving frantically at him. They were signaling that another wave was roaring in. Fred came to his knees and sprint-paddled to meet the next one, made it over the top, and collapsed exhausted. "If it had broken on me I would never have reached shore, but there was Buzzy paddling up looking like a protective human bell buoy. We rested until Buzzy said to follow him. Off we went, back inside to the near shorebreak."

Buzzy led them back down the channel toward shore until he reached the inside line-up. He stroked powerfully for a wave and disappeared down its face. The next Fred saw of his guide was when he walked up on the beach and waved for Fred to come in. Fred sprinted back to the beach, washed up the sand with the shorebreak and waded out to dry land. But where was Al? Buzzy and Fred stood on top of the station wagon searching the choppy waves for a sight of him. They spotted him coming off the crest of a twenty-footer. The wave closed out and Al dropped to a prone position and hung on. Al is a powerful man, strong and heavy, and was able to retain his board. When he got back to the beach he noticed his grip was so firm that his hands had gone right through the fiberglass in two places.

After the boards were racked on the station wagon, Buzzy said, "Let's go to the sanitarium." Both Fred and Al asked what he meant. Buzzy answered, "Makaha. After that encounter out there Makaha will build your egos back to where they belong. Let's get out of here!" They didn't fight the suggestion.

On another day, Fred, George Downing, and Buzzy were searching the North Shore for a spot that was ridable. They had slept very little the previous night. The weather bureau had predicted swells up to twenty-five feet for the North Shore and the surfers were nervously anticipating rough encounters with the waves.

They checked Haleiwa first—impossible. The waves were breaking huge all across the bay and the white water was rolling directly toward the shore six and eight feet high. They went on to Sunset. The same conditions were repeated there. There was nothing left but to explore and try to find a spot where they could paddle out through a channel.

As they were deciding what to do, Bud Browne rolled up in his smoking old Chevy. They joined forces and continued back to Haleiwa. If nothing looked ridable, they could always have a coffee in town and talk about better days. About a mile from town the caravan slowed by an open stretch of beach. They had all passed this spot many times without ever considering the possibility of finding surf. But this morning the waves were different. They were lining up to produce surf, beautiful, fast-peeling-over right slides. It was still a long way from shore, but why not paddle out just for a tester? Bud set up his camera but saw through the view finder that he wasn't high enough to catch the full shape of the wave.

Bud looked around and spotted a big green water tank sitting on the hillside behind the road. As Buzzy and Downing began working their way out to the break, Bud climbed to the tank and set up his tripod and camera. It was a perfect vantage point. He could see Buzzy and George fighting their way out. Off to his right was a little beach house with a sign board reading "Laniakea." An appropriate name for the spot, Bud thought; it meant High Heaven. So was born the now famous Laniakea.

Outside by the Laniakea break, Buzzy stroked down a wave as Bud's camera exposed film on the water tank. Buzzy rode away from the curl to the shoulder and made the wave safely. In the corner of his view finder Bud caught a glimpse of Downing on the same wave but tucked inside the curl. Bud stopped panning and let Downing run into frame. The wave collapsed on George and tons of white wave bashed him away from his board, driving the surfer to the bottom. The white water rose so high it filled the camera's view finder—and to this day that footage is one of the most spectacular wipe-out shots ever filmed at Laniakea.

It was altogether a great day for Buzzy and George. They figured out the ground rules for Laniakea and then tore the place apart. What a discovery they had made! Now they had a marvelous place to surf that would hold a big wave even when Sunset, Waimea and the others were closed out. Buzzy almost blew his mind. He was so jazzed up and happy that he shouted over and over again, "How about it! Another Malibu and twenty feet!" Surf secrets can't be kept in the Islands. Within a week, Laniakea was added to the known surfing breaks. But even today it's still known as Downing's and Buzzy's spot.

Later that same winter, just before spring and the swell-shift that would put the North Shore to bed, Buzzy, Al Wiemers, Pat Curren and Van Dyke sat watching a monstrous west swell tearing apart the Laniakea reef. On a west swell, Laniakea was a ridiculously closed-out spot, but fun to watch. Elsewhere the west swell had ruined surfing for the day. It looked as if the last chance to surf until the following winter had been ruined by the unwanted west swell. They packed up their boards to return to Haleiwa and Marion's Cafe for cups of hot coffee laced with half a dozen lumps of sugar and whitened with canned milk. Sitting in Marion's and drinking the rotten coffee (most cafe-made coffee in Hawaii is terrible) was a depressing climax to what had been a wonderful season.

Buzzy didn't want to give up. He kept looking out the dirty window in the direction of a spot he called Avalanche. Buzzy was the Pied Piper. He read the surf as if it were a book he had written. He looked and looked and suddenly announced, "That's the spot we're going to ride today." They thought no more but followed Buzzy out the door.

The break to which Buzzy was leading them leapt up and over a deep water reef. Avalanche broke only on the biggest of big-wave days, a mile offshore. It was an easy paddle out as the currents flowing from the Haleiwa River swept directly out to sea, but the paddle or swim back was nearly impossible. When the four men neared the line-up, the waves were actually twice the size they had guessed them to be while watching from the beach.

Fred Van Dyke can still remember how it was out at Avalanche: "I don't think I can ever recall being more scared than when I paddled out past the Haleiwa bell buoy a mile from shore. The buoy stands fifteen feet above the level of the sea. From the beach it had only appeared a yard tall. I had seen a wave break right over it from shore. Everywhere huge waves galloped across the bay. I kept paddling out to sea, to deeper water, just for safety. Curren got caught inside. He pushed his board away and dove. That was the last I saw of him until we joined up together on the beach. Wiemers was caught in the currents and was drifting out of sight around the next point.

"Buzzy caught a wave and went in leaving me alone out there. Alone, except that on the other side of the bay and another mile to seaward I could see a huge set moving in toward the bell buoy. I had drifted back inside while watching the other guys. There was no escape. I had to climb over that set. The first one came and I shot up and over, dropping twelve feet down onto its back side. The second wave stood straight up and down as I paddled furiously to get over the crest. Halfway to the top I went over backward, sliding down the wave into the trough as the giant collapsed."

Fred remembers being driven down and around and the light fading and everything growing dark. There was even silence for an instant until the foam caught him and he began churning ferociously. He had lost his sense of equilibrium and swam frantically for the surface, only to run solidly into coral. Fred was trapped in a cave. He had swum in the wrong direction—down in the churning water instead of to the surface. He threw up and began to pass out but somehow the explosively turbulent surge carried him upward and to the air. Somehow Fred reached shore alive. "It would be impossible to describe the ordeal of that swim back to the beach for all I clearly remember afterward is that I swore I would never surf outside Avalanche again, under any conditions, and to this day I have not."

Swimming played a large part in the early efforts to conquer the heavies of the North Shore. Most of the early big-wave riders used to train themselves with extended workouts. In the early 1950's, the majority of surfers were older than today's generation of big-wave riders and took their training very seriously. Tom Zahn, Al Wiemers, Joe Sokolich and other competitive paddlers used to stroke off fifteen miles a day and finish up with a mile swim down the Ala Moana Channel. When the surf was down they would train. This superb conditioning also helped to overcome their psychological fear of big waves. If they knew they were ready physically, then their mental resistance could be overcome.

The swimming workouts at Ala Moana also resulted in its discovery as a surfing spot. A man-made cut in the reef to allow shipping to enter the channel more safely suddenly created a fast-breaking left-slide wall of wave. One day when a bunch of surfers were churning up and down the mile course that Zahn had laid out, Tal Wilson rushed up and called down to the swimmers that the surf was breaking perfectly outside the channel by the harbor

marker. Tal, who holds a master's degree in English and
sold ice cream on the beach at Waikiki, had just been
watching the waves of Ala Moana unfold. He was terribly
excited and urged the surfers to grab their boards and go
out and try the new break.

As they paddled out they could see the waves breaking
like long cylinders of silvery salt. Pat Curren was the first
one to reach the line-up by the striped pole which marked
the harbor entrance. He took off on a straight up-and-down
wall, made the drop and raced off on an eight-foot left
slide. Ala Moana was perfect. It broke so hard and fast it
felt like flying in a wet tunnel.

Now the surfers of the North Shore's winter waves had
found a place that broke to their liking in summer. Ala
Moana was good only during south-swell days, which happened in Hawaii only in summer. But for the excitement of
Tal the ice-cream man, it might have been years before
anyone paddled out to ride Ala Moana.

The winter of 1957 saw the first invasion of the hot-
performing surfers from California. Board design had progressed rapidly and many of the surfers had creative ideas
about how big waves should be ridden. The first group to
try performing in the North Shore surf were Greg Noll,
Mike Stang, Mickey Munoz and Ricky Grigg. There were
others, but these four opened up the whole crazy flirt-with-
the-curl approach. They were also responsible for the final
attack on Waimea Bay which added that place of giant
waves to the list of surfable North Shore breaks.

The North Shore surfers had driven by Waimea Bay
again and again on their hunt for ridable waves, but the
break was far out on the right point and from the road
didn't appear to be worth the hard and dangerous effort to
paddle out. Besides, there was a giant rip that followed
along the shore so strongly that it would carry anyone but
an Olympic swimmer onto the south rocks. There was also
a vicious shorebreak that dumped tons of white water on
the sand each time a wave broke. Waimea just didn't look
worth it.

One day in 1957, Noll, Stang, Munoz and a few others
had watched Waimea breaking for hours. They had
planned their assault carefully. Noll had designed some

special big-wave boards and the crew were impatient to try them out. Greg's boards had thin noses which cut through the chop and released the wind shooting up the face of the wave. The wide tail would make it easier to catch waves and more maneuverable once in the surf. They waxed up and started through the forbidding fifteen-foot shorebreak.

Greg Noll pushed off first. He paddled out during what he considered was a lull, but Greg was not familiar with the speed of the waves that moved into the beach at Waimea. He got caught about a hundred and fifty yards from shore by a huge rolling twenty-footer that had closed out across the channel. Greg's board was ripped away but he made it safely back to the beach.

Mickey Munoz's turn came next. Mickey had learned from Greg's wipe-out, so he waited for a true lull. The pause in the relentless race of waves came and Mickey and Mike Stang raced through the shorebreak to gain the safety of deep open water. As Greg waited on the beach, Pat Curren drove up and joined him. When another quiet period came, they paddled out to join Mickey and Mike Stang. Now there were four out there against the waves of Waimea.

As they pushed their boards out to the line-up, they saw Mickey take off on the first wave that rolled through. What that wave did to Mickey was a revelation. Mickey stood up on the biggest wave any of them had yet seen. Mickey made it to the bottom of the giant, took one look at what was curling over on him and bailed out. Greg started screaming with excitement. That little point wave which appeared from the beach to be just a narrow peak had lined up for two hundred yards and had broken from top to bottom.

Munoz's board popped up out of the five-foot-deep white water and drifted into the channel. Mickey came struggling through the water after it. He looked scared. He didn't say much while paddling back to the line-up, but Greg and the others guessed he'd just had the most frightening experience of his life. Mickey is not a powerhouse. He's tough, capable and aggressive, but being just about five-and-a-half-feet tall limits one's gross strength. The wave that had crushed him was just too much for Mickey. But his experience taught them all one of Waimea's secrets. There was a good chance that a lost board would return to the channel where a swimming surfer could find it and avoid the long swim back followed by a pounding in the shorebreak.

Then the others tried, but with more caution. Soon they caught on and made wave after wave, but only the smaller ones. Here they found a glassy twenty-foot wave with a peaking crest and a rapid out-of-control elevator-like drop.

Later that morning Dr. Don James showed up and pointed his giant telephoto lens at the surfers. The surfers thought they'd give him a chance for a picture of a lifetime. All together they took off. Greg said it didn't seem like much of a wave at first, but then it jumped up steeply over the reef, rising to almost twenty-five feet. Greg was forced to his left instead of to the normal right-slide direction. Since he was on the shoulder, chaos followed. Munoz saw Greg, all two hundred and sixty pounds of him, coming right at him and did the only sane thing. Mickey bailed out. Pat, in his usual cool way, stayed with his board, and Stang held on as long as possible while Greg ploughed into them. They collided. Here were some of the best riders in the world and they were being smashed, eaten alive by that giant Waimea wave. Don James caught the action just before the mix-up. He had a classic still which told the story of Waimea to the others who would follow.

That night, during the inevitable discussion that follows every surfing adventure, they all decided that this had been the steepest take-off in the world. It was almost an impossible wave. The wave had come from deep water with nothing in its way to impede its speed and power. It hit the reef, which was about twenty-five feet below the surface, just as they were coming to their feet. From a swell in the ocean of about twelve feet, the wave jumped almost double. They were not far enough out on the wave and when it leapt, they were left hanging in space and the concavity of the wave took over both surfer and board.

At Waimea, they concluded, there was not time to make a single mistake. Either you calculated and did every move as planned, or you were due for a horrible wipe-out.

The challenge of a thirty-foot Waimea wave still stands.

The day Waimea Bay was conquered. The famous Dr. Don James photo shows
Mike Stang being blown over the top and Pat Curren bailing out.

(Dr. Don James)

Every year, waves thirty feet and higher pour through, but no one has yet successfully descended one. Greg Noll and Mike Stang have probably taken off on the biggest waves at Waimea—monsters just over twenty-five feet—but neither has made it to the bottom still standing.

Greg keeps trying to master Waimea's best. In the winter of 1968, Noll took off on a huge wave. He didn't see someone else who had bailed out and left his board dangling above Greg. The loose board came down. In the mix-up Greg went over, to be hit on the head by his own board. He was knocked unconscious. Ricky Grigg saw the accident and said it looked as if Noll was under a minute and drifted in a good two hundred yards before he popped up. If Greg had not been such a bull of a man and such a floater he might never have survived.

And so Waimea remains the most dangerous of all when the big ones power through. The thirty-foot Waimea wave has yet to be ridden.

John Severson, the publisher of *Surfer* magazine, was one of the early big-wave riders and has contributed much to surfing over the years. During his stay in the army, John had the good luck to be assigned to Hawaii. John had been one of the first to enjoy performing on his native Dana Point waves and he carried his fast-turning style with him to Hawaii. At that time the true big-wave rider had only one desire—to ride as many waves as possible. They trained to Olympic pitch, but didn't care a bit about style. They wanted only to be functional and to achieve as much speed as possible to race the break. John brought a shorter, faster-turning board from California and was one of the first to consider cutting back into the wave and teasing the curl.

He had done this beautifully at Sunset, but his most memorable day came when the big surf of January, 1958, rolled in all the way from Siberia to blast the North Shore's entire length.

John woke up that morning to the sound of thunderous surf breaking off Maili. He got up and looked across the ocean at a vast panorama of white water. Places that had never shown surf before were breaking from top to bottom.

This swell had been tracked from its beginning far across

the Pacific. It had covered thousands of miles on its journey to Hawaii. The weather bureau had sent out warnings,
as the swell was caused by the most extensive low-pressure
system recorded in the Pacific for many years. Usually,
when the weather bureau predicts twelve-foot swells with
fifteen-second intervals, surfers can count on a big-wave
day. This report stated that the swells were twenty-one
feet with twenty-five-second intervals—almost a record.

John grabbed his movie camera and board and ground
up the Farrington Highway to Makaha. The road at that
time led to the country and the little farms. There were no
park facilities or hotels then, just the surfers sleeping on
the beach or in ragged pup tents.

Makaha was almost completely closed out. There it was,
that famous surf which had drawn him again and again.
Out on the water were Buzzy and Downing. A few others
sat beyond the huge break, watching. John waxed and
paddled out. It took him a good twenty minutes to reach
the far point. He could see Pat Curren and Downing edg-
ing in trying to pick up a smaller wave, but they wisely
backed off. It was simply impossible—but nobody had told
that to Severson. Later, Buzzy described one wave he tried
as being so fast that as he shot through the curl onto the
seeming safety of the shoulder, the wave folded and caught
him from behind. This convinced the experts. They'd sit
and watch for awhile.

Severson didn't realize what was happening and continued to paddle for the nonexistent bowl where the normal
big-wave start was made. Usually, the Makaha bowl was
the gigantic climax to the wave; this was where one
climbed high and rode through the exploding surf into the
channel and safety. George Downing likes to tell of seeing
fish floating around in the bowl, stunned into unconscious-
ness by the falling wave. The sharks would then gather for
a dinner of knocked-out fish—or a possible surfer. John,
however, had none of the fear, or knowledge, gained from
years of surfing Makaha that Buzzy, Downing and the
others had.

John saw a huge one coming around the point and
started paddling. Buzzy saw the same swell building and
turned around and paddled out to sea. His judgment told

him this was a sure death wave. But John kept going. No one told him.

The wave came and John caught it, catapulted down the face of the giant and made a bottom turn. He didn't have time for anything else. The whole gigantic wave, the tons and tons of cascading water poured down on him. He was driven deep, to bounce off the bottom in thirty feet of water. Buzzy said he counted to thirty, slowly, before John came up. And John remembers feeling his ribs cracking, and passing out on his way to the surface. Being under the water for even fifteen seconds is unusual, even at Waimea or Sunset. Later, after a heated discussion on the beach, they all agreed that the wave was very close to thirty feet high, the biggest wave any of the men of the North Shore had yet attempted.

There were days at Makaha when the surf didn't rise and there was time for other pleasures. One of the men who added much to the good times—his name has now been forgotten—was the Makaha Brew Maker. Along the wilderness-like beach, this strange individual would make his beer in clay pots. As the evil broth fermented in the sun, the flies would gather to sip the bubbling liquid, be overcome by the fumes, and die, to float in the scum.

There were nights when the Makaha group would head for the Wainai movie house—open to the stars and mosquitos. This was Buzzy's favorite way of spending the evening. Buzzy, Chuck King, and Walt Hoffman would often be the only *haoles* sitting on the wooden benches. Most of the feature pictures shown then were old World War II movies, and the predominantly Japanese audience would cheer and clap as the airplanes with the rising sun on their wing tips strafed the downed American flyers floating in the life rafts. Ultimately John Wayne would triumph and the Japanese villains would be shot down in flames and crash into the sea. The audience would sullenly grumble and Buzzy would say, "Listen to 'em, listen to 'em, they don't like that part!" Then it was back to Makaha and a night under the stars and the surf that would be waiting at dawn.

Two marvelous people, true individuals, round out the old big-wave crew of the North Shore—Peter Cole and Walt Hoffman. Both are fine watermen who are still surfing. Pete stands out because he was fearless and Walt because he had all the fears one could have of the big surf but still rode the very largest.

For many years Peter Cole was Mr. North Shore. It was often hard to decide which of the really great surfers came first—but the top three would certainly be Buzzy, Peter and Ricky Grigg; since the order of rank shifted daily, there was really no number one.

Peter Cole was an individualist, whether in the water, on the beach, or teaching his class. He did the impossible. The normal fears of drowning, being caught in rips, not making it under a huge wave, were not a part of Pete's make-up. He could do almost anything in the water and was one of the strongest swimmers ever to stroke in from the Waimea rip. The only fear Peter ever had was that someone might ride a bigger wave or take off in a more critical spot. Fred Van Dyke remembers when he made the mistake of starting down ahead of Peter on a good-size Waimea wave: "As I dropped in I caught a glimpse of Peter behind me on the shoulder side. I should have known better but I was committed. He rode up high, passed me and shot on. It scared me but I stood, angled, and my board dropped out and sailed through space. Then I landed on top of it and rolled off to the side as the wave sucked me feet first down its face and then catapulted me into thin air. The whole thing caved in on top of me. I survived but when I surfaced I saw my board split in two, double stringer, four layers of fiberglass, and all."

The contest at Waimea was usually between Peter, Pat Curren, Greg Noll, Mike Stang, and Jose Angel. What usually happened was that they all ended up taking off on some out-of-sight point wave and were totally smashed when the wave folded a hundred yards closer to the beach.

Pete was sometimes a loner and would paddle out to the big ones by himself. A typical Cole adventure was to arrive at Waimea late in the afternoon when the wind blowing over from Khuku created a confused five-foot cross-chop, and go surfing alone.

One day Peter had a witness to his early evening surfing. Fred Van Dyke had pulled up to check Waimea and found Pete waxing up and ready to go out. All Peter said as he

A close-out wave at Sunset Beach. Every surfer has abandoned ship, diving under the break to escape being sucked into the falling tons of white water.

(Dr. Don James)

looked out to a set of choppy twenty-footers was, "That can be surfed," and off he paddled.

When Peter reached the point he looked like an ant on that heaving sea. He took off on a few smaller waves as a form of warm up and then paddled out to where the biggest were spilling over in storm-tossed confusion. A huge set swung around the point and Peter positioned himself and began to paddle. "From shore it looked easy until I saw the chop swinging across the wave like a giant snake," Van Dyke recalled. "Peter began his slide and stood up, and then the chop reached his wave and hit him full blast. His board turned completely and Peter fell through space and hit the trough just before the wave broke. It sucked him halfway up the face and then let go. He looked more like a derelict of some kind than a human being. Peter hit in a cannon-ball tuck and I did not see him pop up until he was a hundred yards inside where he'd been buried."

It's hard to imagine how tough and strong a waterman Peter Cole was. He survived that horribly crunching wipeout and swam in against a rip moving seaward at ten knots, while fighting a wind that was blowing offshore a good twenty-five miles an hour—and he could do this hour after hour and day after day. The perfect physical man? No, Peter is almost blind without his glasses.

Walt Hoffman had been a competitive swimmer and could handle himself beautifully in California's surf, but the North Shore was tough on him. Walt was a big and loud surfer, somewhat fat, but sleek in the water—like a long seal with plenty of blubber. He would bluster and catcall and want everyone around to know he'd ride the biggest; this was his way of bucking himself up, his own type of banzai-charge morale builder.

In spite of his large frame he was a beautiful, graceful surfer. He introduced many of the newer boards to the Islands and brought his own California style and adapted it to big surf. Walt could also learn from the others with experience of the North Shore. He needed every bit of advice and all the tricks of surviving to encourage him to tackle the big ones. One day at Sunset when conditions were horrible and the strong offshore winds were making everyone nervous, Walt drove up screaming, "Hey, you guys want big surf?" Then follow me!" He drove off and the caravan followed. Walt led them to a spot about a mile up from Sunset. After they had parked and climbed from their old fifty-dollar-per-body surf cars, Walt bellowed again, "See! Out there, see that surf! Not that stuff way outside, but the break on the inside reef. Surf that! Simmons showed it to me back in '52." And with another yell he led the gang out.

Walt always knew someplace to try and surf when the regular spots were flat or blown out or even too dangerous for the top surfers. The spot Walt had led them to turned out to be quite good and as the years passed it became known as "Velzyland."

The good years of the big surf continued and more and more people began hearing just how great it was on the North Shore. The early surf films and the first few issues of the surf magazines elaborated on the fascination of big waves. As the planes came in from California with their surfboard-carrying passengers the North Shore began to change.

Instead of knowing everyone carrying a surfboard on top of his car, the old pioneers began seeing hundreds of younger faces that didn't smile or wave at them. It was soon apparent that there was a surfer population explosion taking place on Oahu's North Shore. The younger surfers attacked the heavies like their leaders had done, but there was a change. They were not as wary. Wipe-outs were still the big subject of after-surfing conversation, but the deep, underlying fear of the unknown was rapidly dying.

The weather bureau was also becoming surf-conscious. It was able to predict storms four or five days distant and state almost to the foot the height of the waves and how long the surf would last. Now the surfers called the weather bureau for information. In the old days it was the other way round.

The old crew of big-wave riders really wasn't interested in smaller, fun-sized waves and would often rack their boards when the size dropped below eight feet. But the newcomers, the hot-dogging performers, began to glory in the smaller and faster waves. Pupukea, an excellent small-wave break, opened up to the young Californians first.

Some of the kids surfing the Pipeline took a walk up the beach and discovered Chun's and Piddlies and others that the old-timers had never bothered to ride before. It was beautiful warm-water California surf, but a little bigger and faster, and the kids from the mainland began ripping it apart.

The news of the new spots spread rapidly and the atmosphere began changing. The beaches began to resemble contest day at Huntington Beach, and more and more tourists came out from Honolulu dropping their film wrappers and Kleenex tissues. The virginity of the newly discovered spots lessened daily. The tides cleaned the beaches now and then, but even nature couldn't keep up with the avalanche of newcomers.

Then came the camera explosion. Bud Browne's films had been a tremendous hit in California and other cameramen flew across to make their own surf slicks. Severson was there first, then came Walt Philips, Grant Rohlof, Dale Davis, Jim Freeman, Greg MacGilivary, Bruce Brown and Don Brown, and at least three others who made one movie and dropped out. Surf films were pouring out and only Kodak and Bruce Brown grew richer. There was one day at Sunset when the cameras on the beach outnumbered the surfers in the waves. As these films were released the young audiences would become more and more turned on by the wonderful quality and beauty of Hawaiian surf and would hop the first jet they could for the Islands.

Most of the newly arrived didn't have sufficient experience and many got into trouble in the surf and among the swift-flowing rips. The local citizens of the North Shore became so tired of saving the victims off their front yards that they formed a rescue squad.

The second wave of young surfers from California, and later from the Atlantic Coast, came better prepared. These were the young pros hardened by several seasons of contest experience. This period saw the Mike Doyles, the David Nuuhiwas, the Steve Biglers arriving with sponsors supporting them. They came as unofficial board salesmen riding a brand-name surfboard to give the builder publicity. These surfers threw caution to the winds. They rode as free individuals and tore the waves—both large and small—

apart. For some reason they didn't have the fear, the hang-up that handicapped the old pioneers. Perhaps it was because they started earlier and someone had already blazed the way for them to follow through the rips and currents.

What had started out as a desire by the pioneers to get away from the crowd, to be individuals, to escape the tensions of society, turned out to be the "in" thing to do. The surf society that developed excluded the pioneers. Many of them left the Islands. Some even quit surfing, while others, like Cole and Buzzy, George Downing and Jose Angel, made the adjustment into the modern world of surfing.

The real end of the days of pioneering and male surf heroes came when women like Marge Calhoun, Linda Benson and Joyce Hoffman paddled out with the big-wave riders and stayed to compete for surf space. Linda Benson rode Waimea one day and did better than some of the men. Joyce handled Sunset beautifully up to twelve feet, and Marge Calhoun, almost a grandmother by then, rode Makaha on a blistering fifteen-foot day as well as all but a few of the experts like Buzzy and George Downing. It was another shock to see Pete Peterson and a pretty young girl sliding tandem at Sunset on a twelve-foot day. On another day at Makaha, Robin Grigg rode wave-for-wave with her brother, Ricky.

Then came the very young, whom the old-timers regarded as little boys. Jeff Hackman and Jock Sutherland, both from Hawaii, began riding Pipeline and Sunset when they were twelve years old. Today, still in their teens, Jeff and Jock are doing things in big surf that would have been thought impossible ten years before.

One day recently, Peter Cole and Fred Van Dyke were surfing Ala Moana near Honolulu. They had come in to rest, leaving some of their students behind to continue riding. Van Dyke remarked that surfing was falling apart like themselves. It was time to rack their boards and let the young take over. As the discussion about age and retirement grew heated, some of the kids paddled in and edged up to listen. Peter was arguing that the surf wasn't as big as it used to be. He was shaking his head and throwing his arms about for emphasis when one of his contact lenses worked loose and fell into the sand. Peter dropped down on the sand and began groveling for the precious lens. After ten minutes of fruitless searching, Pete came up with what he thought was an ingenious idea. The trade winds were blowing at ten knots. If a gust of wind caught the other lens, it would carry it to the same place where the first was lost. Peter took out the other contact lens and dropped it. The wind carried it away and down to the sand. He never found either.

Pete's students still talk about his logic and his surfing ability and his contact with reality. That's about where most of the early surfing heroes are at this point in history —digging about in the sand trying to find something precious that is lost. They had served their purpose. It was time to move aside before they crumbled into antiquity. No one could take away their spirit and what they had found, but the kings were dead. Long live the kings.

CHAPTER 6

Ricky Grigg—Surfer, Scientist

The swells would arrive and lift me to their mountain
tops. Then they'd pass and drop me into deep valleys.
It was almost like night in the troughs. Just being out
there, a mile offshore, with all that force was beautiful.
It was the biggest thrill I've ever had.

Ricky Grigg

From Peru, from Florida, from Australia, California and
Hawaii, twenty-four of the world's best surfers came to
ride in the "Duke" contest. They were all top wave men
and were all invited to participate by the Duke himself.
Among them was a quiet-spoken, partly-bald oceanographer. He was a good surfer, but some wondered why
he was invited—he'd never won a major contest and had
almost given up surfing competition. But the Duke knew
who were the real champions and he had insisted that
twenty-nine-year-old Ricky Grigg be included. The old
Hawaiian's judgment of the surf and surfers was sure—he
had picked the winner even before the start of the contest.
What the spectators at the Duke's contest saw was grandeur in the surf—a complete upset and a victory for a
very wave-wise, competitive scientist-sportsman.

The world of Ricky Grigg is perhaps the ideal combina-
tion of intellect, science and action. Few men have been
so fortunate. One of our last frontiers, the sea, is Ricky's
professional office, his source of income, and his playing
field. The sea is as natural a working place for Rick as is

the engineer's drafting table or the stockbroker's booth. As a graduate student at Scripps Institution of Oceanography at La Jolla, Ricky has frequent opportunity to work on and under the sea. Last year Ricky was a member of Team Number III of the U.S. Navy's Man-Under-the-Sea project. He lived in the deep water, over two hundred feet down off San Diego, for fifteen days. The summer before Sea-Lab, he was deep-diving for the rare black coral of Hawaii. Several summers before that, Ricky was saving lives as a Santa Monica, California, beach lifeguard. Ricky has been a competitive swimmer and surfer most of his adult life. While in junior college he won All-America status as a sprint swimmer.

Rick is not the usual hot-surfer who follows the California surf-meet trail from spring to fall and goes on to Hawaii for the winter heavies. He has entered very few meets and had won only once before his victory at Sunset Beach. What was important, though, was that Ricky had been surfing big waves consistently. This kind of practice was invaluable; whenever Ricky could escape from his Ph. D. program, he made the tourist-section flight to Honolulu. Unlike the tourists, he didn't stop at Waikiki but went directly to the North Shore and the waves of Sunset Beach.

To win in big, powerful Sunset surf, the rider needs three qualifications: experience and intense desire to win; luck; and almost perfect skill in judging waves. Ricky had all three working for him the day he paddled out with twenty-three of the world's best surfers. Again and again he placed himself in just the right position for the best waves. His rides were both calculated and daring. He seemed to know just how far to slide onto the tunneling crests and just when to burst out and make for the clear water. His graceful bravado impressed the judges and he rolled up two hundred and fifty-three points against a possible three hundred—twenty-four points ahead of second-place Mike Doyle, one of the most consistent winners in the surfing world.*

After the meet Ricky was really "stoked." Before the

---

* Surfers are scored on the five best waves they ride in each heat. In the finals Grigg rode ten waves, receiving perfect scores on two of them.

official scores were tabulated several experienced wave watchers rushed to congratulate him. Rick couldn't believe he'd won. He admitted he was hot and every ride felt good, but he was up against the very best. Ricky felt it was Felipe Pomar, the Peruvian champion, who'd won, or possibly Doyle. When the scores came in and Ricky was officially the winner he still couldn't believe it at first. But it was true. The slightly balding doctor-to-be in oceanography had just found himself crowned the world's best surfer. He said, "Even if I'd come in fifteenth I'd still feel like a winner—every man who surfed here today is a champion."

Thousands of waves have passed under Ricky and hundreds of thousands of pages from text books have passed beneath his eyes. Both the waves and the books have influenced the life of this unique young man. Only by taking a closer look at Ricky can we understand what it takes to create a surfing champion and a man of science.

Ricky's love affair with the sea began at State Beach, Santa Monica Canyon, California. This beach, second only to Malibu for oddball happenings and offbeat characters, was where Ricky's older sister, Robin, pulled him out of the surf when he was two years old. His parents decided after that tumble in the waves that it was time for Ricky to learn to swim. The lessons paid off and Ricky took to the water from then on—as a surfer, oceanographer, aquanaut, oarsman, commercial skin diver, beach lifeguard, and competitive swimmer.

Wave judgment, which Ricky has mastered to perfection, started at old State Beach where he learned to capture the force of a nature-made wave and send his body sliding toward the beach. When you're not yet five feet tall, weigh less than fifty pounds, and are only eight years old, it's important to judge how an incoming wave will break. If you misjudge and a powerful sandbuster cracks over you, the results can be both dangerous and frightening. After a dozen or two harsh encounters with hard-breaking waves, Ricky learned what could be bodysurfed—and what couldn't. He'd mastered the first lesson of surfmanship.

Ricky wrapped his hands around his first surfboard at the age of eleven. His three years of background in competitive swimming gave him the confidence he needed to surf well at such an early age.

Ricky and Buzzy Trent, an old friend and still Ricky's number one surf hero, started riding the waves of State Beach together. State's beach-break waves called for fast reactions and rapid turning which wasn't easy on the heavy boards the kids were surfing then.

One morning before the swimmers arrived for the day, Ricky and Buzzy were cranking their old balsas around in the shorebreak. Somehow they got their signals crossed and instead of both going left or right they came straight at each other. In the collision that followed, Ricky's board spun out. The nose came up and caught him in the stomach. The result—a ruptured spleen that had to be removed. The extensive operation kept Ricky in the hospital for several weeks, but the day he was released he and Buzzy headed for Palos Verdes. They figured the surf would be gentle and Ricky could ride safely. When they arrived at the beach the waves were up. They went out and on the first wave Ricky took a bad wipe-out and out popped all the stitches. It was back to hospital.

The wound finally healed and Ricky was released. This time he had learned, and waited until the doctor gave him permission to surf again. The accident didn't slow Ricky down one bit. He kept on surfing, but the long scar still remains as a constant reminder of how powerful a loose board and a small wave can be when they mix. Ricky would advance to become one of the best and youngest of the big-wave riders, but first came his wave apprenticeship.

Malibu was Ricky's next training ground. At that time, 1950, the beach at Malibu was still relaxed and free of the frenzy that was to come. The hut was yet to be built and the parties starting at sundown were nothing but wiener roasts over a driftwood fire. The three youngest riding Malibu then were Buzzy Trent, Ricky, and Mickey Dora—all in their early teens, the youngest of the Malibu surfing fellowship.

Then the Malibu scene began for Ricky. He was caught up in the turbulent backwash of Malibu's beach life. As Ricky remembers, "I was there before all the mystique business. Then came Tube Steak, the hut, and the guys

All time Hawaiian pioneer surfer, Buffalo Keaulana, competes at Makaha, 1966.
(P. L. Dixon)

who started living there and Malibu became pretty grubby. I became engrossed in it. I was fourteen and fifteen and became involved in what turned out to be an ugly situation. Malibu wasn't a good influence. There was no authority or direction and no elders the young kids could follow or look to with respect. I had to climb to get out of it. I had to make a decision and I was lucky. I made it out."

Ricky turned to competitive swimming and water polo and churned his way to a spot on the Junior Olympics team. Next came Santa Monica City College and beach lifeguarding. As a guard Ricky participated in all the water sports activities of the busy Southern California summer aquatic season. There were paddle-polo games, ocean-swimming races, dory racing and the Intercity Lifeguard Games—and skin diving early in the morning before work. It was almost like being a fish. Ricky's interest in the sea grew beyond sports and, because his mind is innately curious, he began reading and studying about the forces of nature that bring the grunion, produce the red tides, deliver the swells that make surf, and cause the lobster to be the way it is.

This was his turning point, the period in his life when he decided that the ocean was to be his career. But Ricky couldn't give up surfing. It meant too much. How to combine this love of the waves with academic study became his persistent conflict.

Ricky entered Santa Monica City College and, under the guidance of Coach John Joseph, trained to become one of the top California swimmers of the day. The two years of junior college had a settling effect on him. He felt a need for a more challenging school that would offer a bachelor's degree. He transferred to Stanford University. Stanford can be a rough transition after the easy ways of a junior college, but it was close to the waves of Santa Cruz. If he kept his grades up, there would be surfing on holidays and weekends, and Santa Cruz has some of the biggest waves on the Pacific Coast.

Ricky graduated from Stanford. Along with his degree he picked up two good seasons of surfing the exciting cold-water waves of Santa Cruz. Ricky then asked himself, "Now where? The next school has to be by the ocean, where I can study marine biology and find even bigger surf."

Ricky had never forgotten his first visit to the Islands the summer he was sixteen. Hawaii and the big surf of the North Shore kept pulling at him to cross the Pacific. The first black and blurry photographs of Sunset and Waimea Bay were starting to arrive in California. The reports brought back by Simmons and Joe Quigg and a few of the other California surfers were exciting and causing a lot of young men to start planning for a big-wave trip to Hawaii. Ricky gave in to his deep yearning, packed, and left for Oahu and the University of Hawaii and his eventual master's degree.

It was both the big surf and the Department of Marine Zoology at the University of Hawaii that motivated Ricky to emigrate for five years to Hawaii. He'd had his kicks over and over again riding Southern California's waves, but the compulsion for the giants of the North Shore didn't become overpowering until he had his first wet taste of really big surf at Rincon.

Rincon, near Santa Barbara, California, comes up number one of all the West Coast big-wave spots. On a good sunny winter day the surfer driving north to Rincon can see the long beautiful lines of swells marching in with almost military precision from over three miles down the road. Way out, perhaps a half mile off Rincon Point, a small speck of a surfer will take off on a howling breaker. If he's good and the wave holds, that little speck will race for shore and grow and grow until he becomes an individual locked so tight into the curl that it's almost impossible to believe he'll ever get out.

Ricky arrived at Rincon early in the morning of one of the once-every-ten-or-twelve-years super-surf days. Surfers who were there still talk about that January 10th of 1953 when Rincon began breaking an unbelievable twenty feet. Ricky says, "There were sets that day that came rolling in so fast and so huge it was simply fantastic. On that same day waves were breaking in water thirty- to forty-feet deep in Santa Monica Bay, which means from an oceanographic standpoint that the waves had to be twenty-five feet high. At Rincon only six of us got out. Mat Kivlin, Joe Quigg, Kit Horn, Bobby Petterson, and Bev Morgan and myself. It was so special, like my destiny had been marked that day. I overcame the great fear the waves inspired. I came out of my shell. I knew I had to head for Hawaii. Hawaii didn't have to come right away, there was school first. But later, that one day at Rincon stayed deep in my memory to keep nagging at me. After high school I gave in to the urge and went off to Hawaii. I'd guess you could say that Rincon, that fabulous 10th of January, started me toward both oceanography and my individual hang-up with the big surf."

Ricky could be called a born big-wave rider. He just doesn't feel comfortable in surf under eight and ten feet. As he says, "I feel like some sort of kook until the waves reach a certain size, say twelve feet. After that there's enough room to command the situation and I begin to feel loose on the board." Ricky became very serious about big waves. During his five years in the Islands he tried to develop a new style of big-wave surfing.

The first of the big-wave riders were take off, drop in, and race-away-from-the-break specialists. With their long and fast big-gun boards they were limited to this approach. Ricky began to observe that there was more to big-wave riding than just making the wave and avoiding falling. For five years he developed his performing style in big waves. He began experimenting with better board equipment, shortening the length so he could turn and cut back into the curl. Ricky's theories proved correct. He was able to do more than the pioneers. In fact he was a pioneer himself, taking surfing another step along the way. Today, most of the current big-wave riders are performing, hot-dogging, and staying closer and closer to the break the way Ricky proved it could be done.

In September of 1958, Ricky began his five-year residence in Hawaii. His arrival was also the beginning of the modern period of big-wave surfing. It was Ricky and Peter Cole together who showed the pioneers that their scene could be improved upon, that the waves weren't as fear-inspiring as they thought and that the treacherous currents and rips of the North Shore could be handled. Peter and

Ricky were excellent watermen and two of the fastest and strongest competitive swimmers of California during that period. Their first winter in the Islands started off slowly until around the middle of October when Sunset began to pour through. And then it all began.

The old-timers would watch Peter and Ricky paddle out together to the farthest part of the peak, even to the other side of it on some days. There, each would fight for position. They were beautiful in their innocence of wipe-out fear. Up until the time of Ricky and Peter, the early big-wave surfers worried seriously about whether they would make it back to shore when they lost their boards.

Aside from Jim Fisher and Mike Stang, none of the early group were competitive swimmers and thus they lacked that fine edge of technique that only years of practice and coaching can bring. Most of the initiators of big-wave riding regarded the North Shore as treacherous because of the swift rips and the rapidly-changing surf conditions that would suddenly bring huge close-out sets roaring in from nowhere. At first they tried never to surf alone and made promises to retrieve each other's boards. They had fins in their cars for swimming out into the channels for lost boards. Endless conferences were held on how to handle a bad wipe-out and the ensuing swim through the bone-crushing shorebreaks.

Peter and Ricky, both being half fish, laughed at the timidity of the originators, and the stage was set for the most competitive and fiercely beautiful surfing battles yet seen on the North Shore. What followed set the standards of modern big-wave riding and established the pattern of today's daring-dangerous surfing.

Peter and Ricky really shook the dyed-in-the-wool surfers of the old North Shore with their disdainful attitudes. The pair were simply not concerned with a wipe-out. One day at Waimea, Ricky was taking off on a huge wave, well over fifteen feet high, when he suddenly got so jazzed over the beauty of the curling monster that he ran to the nose of his board, screamed with delight and then unexpectedly dove off the nose of the board. He landed prone down the face of the wave in a body-surfing position and kept on going. Fred Van Dyke was paddling out to the break and remembers seeing the whole thing: "Ricky shot down and body-surfed across the face of the wave like a sea lion. He didn't have swim fins and couldn't keep ahead of the break. Suddenly, in the middle of the steepest part of the wave, he spun out and bounced down to the trough to be engulfed by tons of white water. I retrieved his board and asked him why. 'Aw gee, Fred, the wave was so beautiful that I just couldn't do anything else.' That's the kind of guy Ricky was when he went out in big waves."

On the same day Peter Cole took off on a far outside point wave which stood straight up to twenty-five feet. His board, just under ten feet, couldn't handle the angle. He had done everything perfectly, but his wave was too much. The board dropped out from beneath Peter and left him facing the wave and clawing at the mountain hanging above. It was almost like slow motion. Then gravity took over. Peter took the wipe-out and swam in with no trouble at all and the locals stood amazed. Peter and Ricky went on to open the whole big-wave thing so wide that when they'd finished a couple of seasons there wasn't much left to be done.

The Cole-Grigg team also decided Sunset could be hotdogged, and had Pat Curren shape them two boards around nine and a half feet long, very short by the standards of those days. On their first day out they became so stoked at working over Sunset that they stayed until darkness and physical exhaustion forced them in.

On one of the first Sunset waves ever hot-dogged, Ricky dropped back into the tube and was lost from sight for five seconds. He then trimmed for speed, busted out of the tunnel, and came screaming across the wave's face in a crouch with one hand holding the rail. Peter Cole was on the same wave and Rick's ride so excited the bigger man that he dropped down from the top of the wave right on his partner and then raced in front. Peter's wake caused Ricky to start to fall and Peter slowed, allowed Ricky to draw abreast, and then reached out to grab his friend and hold him up. Peter continued to hold Ricky while they shot along the rest of the wave and rode the white water to the beach. That ended the competition for the day, each agreeing that for once it had been a draw.

The stories about the friendly rivalry between Grigg and Cole are endless. Many of the incidents had the slow, subtle Cole humor mixed with a trace of irony.

Peter had just won the Makaha Championships and that evening had brought his huge trophy home to the beach house he shared with Ricky. Ricky had also competed but had not done as well. As soon as Peter came home he hung the trophy over Rick's bed—as an unspoken golden reminder of who had won that day.

One day at Maili, below Makaha, when a huge west swell was running, a group of surfers had parked just to watch the giants bowl over more than a mile from shore. Most of them had never seen Maili break so big, though George Downing, Woody Browne, Dave Mojas and Wally Froiseth were familiar with the far outside break and had named it Cloud Break. Ricky wanted to see what it looked like up close. The older surfers warned him that it was more than a mile out and that what looked like twenty feet from the beach might well be above thirty feet outside.

But Rick had made up his mind and paddled out. Some thousand-yards seaward he stopped. Waves were breaking in front of where he bobbed. Rick told the group later that he wondered whether he was going to have to push through all that wet power. The waves backed off and he continued to paddle out to the line-up. The wind began to change and the wave shape shifted and became critically dangerous. Rick got one ride and came in. He had gone out under extremely adverse conditions to waves he'd never experienced before, with the possible chance of running into dangerous sharks. In the event of a wipe-out there was also the danger of being swept by parallel currents into the rocks of Keana Point—and all that merely on a whim to see up close just how big the surf was.

It was this same kind of attitude that prompted Ricky, Jose Angel, Greg Noll, Bob Pike and Max Lim to attempt the never-before-ridden "Outside Pipeline." Only on days of big surf does the far-out Pipeline break show, and on this day in January, '62, the outside reef was causing the swells to crest over a good eighteen feet plus.

Jose Angel was the first out and took off on the first wave that rolled in. Bud Browne was on the beach shooting

These are the endless lines of swells that make Sunset Beach, Oahu,
almost the place of the perfect wave.

(Ron Church)

stills and caught a fantastic picture of Jose dropping down the front and being buried. The photo showed the wave to be eighteen feet. Ricky took the next one, which walled over and caught him. He was completely smothered. Another man was blasted off and washed down to Pupukea a half mile away. The rest of the surfers stayed on the beach. Even Max Lim, a paddling competitor, couldn't get through to reach the Outside Pipeline. Those who did took such punishment, they gave up. But the word was out and surging along the bamboo telegraph that the Outside Pipeline had been ridden by Ricky and Jose. Soon, others came on better days and Outside Pipeline was ridden again and again.

The "Banzai Pipeline" had that special magic that captured the interests of surfers and the surf-following public. By the next season came songs and recordings about the Pipeline—and the new and younger surfing stars who would ride it for the grinding cameras of the surf-film makers.

And the Pipeline took its fee, its toll in broken boards and injured surfers. Probably no other surfing spot in the Islands has gained so much fame, created and destroyed so many reputations, and caused so many broken bones. Peruvian Shigi Quesada died there. On any eight- to ten-foot day you can see people swimming in who have been smashed against the bottom, losing teeth, breaking their jaws, tearing their scalps open. Jose Angel has had dozens of stitches taken in his head. Bob Pike dislocated and broke his collarbone. Greg Noll has had at least five boards snapped apart in the fierce shorebreak. Fred Hemmings Jr. took such a crunching wipe-out pushing through that he was shaken and white-faced for days afterwards—and Fred is one of the toughest of the North Shore crew.

Hawaii was Rick's home from '58 until '63, when he entered Scripps Institution of Oceanography to work for his doctor's degree in marine biology. In the Islands, Ricky finished his graduate work and earned his master's degree in marine zoology. He toiled at night on the docks as a longshoreman, taught school at famous Punahou, dove for black coral two hundred feet down off Maui for a year, and of course surfed whenever the waves came up. Black-coral diving proved so fascinating that Ricky decided to study the rare coral as the subject for his thesis. To find the coral, which makes beautiful jewelry and brings a good profit to the diver, requires an underwater hunt which takes the harvester to extreme depths. Ricky and the others who dove for the coral used self-contained underwater breathing apparatus—SCUBA.

Prolonged stays at depths below sixty feet can result in a painful and possibly fatal case of decompression sickness (called "the bends"). It takes just five minutes at the two-hundred-foot level to absorb sufficient nitrogen for the bends to develop when the diver returns to the surface. Thus, every dive Ricky and the others made was potentially dangerous. Here's how Ricky almost packed it up on one such coral-harvesting descent: "I'd been hacking away at a big branch of black coral and had just got it loose. So I wouldn't lose it to the currents I had to drag the branch up the slope of the reef and tie it to the anchor so it could be hauled to the surface. The anchor was thirty yards away from where I'd cut the coral. By the time I reached the anchor and tied the branch to it I was starting to puff and the air was gone.

"I reached for the reserve lever and gave it a tug only to discover that it had been tripped somehow and my reserve air was gone. I ran out of air at two hundred feet, just completely flat out. There wasn't even a half breath left. There was no time to do anything but push off the bottom and scratch for the surface. If I hadn't been panting I could have dropped my scuba and made an easy free ascent, but I was so hungry for air that the need for it became more than desperate." Ricky made the top almost unconscious and was the closest he has ever come to drowning.

The underwater world has held almost as compelling a fascination for Ricky as has surfing. While undergoing the difficult graduate program at Scripps, Ricky had a chance to participate in the underwater-scientific adventure of a lifetime—as one of the elite aquanauts in the Navy's Man-Under-The-Sea program.

Sealab I and II were America's first attempts to prove that man can live and work under the sea for prolonged periods. The French, under the energetic leadership of Jacques Cousteau, had been the first to live underwater in their Conshelf Habitat beneath the Red Sea. The U.S. Navy would go the French one better and deeper.

The first attempt was Sealab I, an underwater station set on the bottom of the Caribbean thirty miles off Bermuda. Four divers inhabited the underwater shelter for eleven days, a hundred and ninety-three feet below the surface.

Sealab II was planned for La Jolla Canyon, a deep underwater cleft lying just offshore from Scripps Institution of Oceanography. The cigar-shaped lab would be moored two hundred and five feet deep near the mouth of the undersea canyon. Three teams would man the station, each staying below for fifteen days. Ricky was selected as a member of Team III. His position as the crew's marine biologist required him to measure bottom currents and study the fish-life food chain and the feeding and behavioral habits of the underwater creatures surrounding the lab.

The only practical way to study the marine environment firsthand was to leave the lab, get out among the fish. So Ricky made daily swimming forays in and out of his aquatic home. Sounds ideal. Just duck out of the lab's open-to-the-sea hatch, swim around with the fish and return to dryness two hundred and five feet from the air and sunlight above.

But they couldn't surface. Ricky and the other aquanauts were living in a special atmosphere of helium, nitrogen, and oxygen. This breathing mixture had become so saturated in their tissue and blood that an unplanned ascent would cause them to suffer a certain and horrible death.

Each journey from Sealab had to be carefully planned to avoid becoming lost, because when the air in their scubas ran out it was surface or drown. It was like reverse mountain climbing. The divers leaving the lab would carry along lights, and tie yellow plastic guide lines to the structure in order to find their way back. To be forced to the surface was the worst danger the swimmers faced. Ricky remembers worrying about it. "If lost outside of Sealab most divers would have just kept swimming and enjoyed what time they had left, because it would be less painful to drown than be forced to surface and start rupturing internally. We knew that every cell in our bodies would have burst on the surface."

Life inside the lab wasn't all comfort and enjoyment either. The divers suffered from the excessive moisture. Their skin developed persistent rashes and the breathing mixture sometimes became polluted with carbon monoxide, causing pounding headaches and nausea.

When they returned to the surface, they were all proud of the part they'd played in extending man's environment to the depths of the sea. As Scott Carpenter, the team leader, shook Ricky's hand on the surface, the surfer-aquanaut winced. Ricky had been stung twice on the hand and once in the foot by poison-spined scorpion fish—the only injuries he suffered during his weeks below the sea.

Ricky would prefer not to be characterized as just a surfer who rides big waves well. If he could have only one title it would be "Man of the Sea." Ricky has become deeply wedded to the sea, not just to the swells and waves that move over the surface but to the total ocean environment. The sea to Ricky offers so much: "Being a part of the ocean, swimming, diving, surfing, rowing, collecting what drifts up on the beach—the whole thing has made the sea kind of a mother to me. The sea absorbs me and provides every kind of passion I know. There's intense interest, excitement, love, fear, deep respect. Because the sea offers so much to study, so many emotional and physical thrills, the sea is very personal to me."

To Ricky the waves are just the skin of the ocean: "There's so much more: the currents, the marine life, the geology—learning about all this makes you feel like a part of evolution. After all the sea is where we came from. The oceans and all they contain have given a unity to my life. The sea is consistent. It will always be there."

In the sea Ricky finds the same struggle for life that goes on behind the waves, on the beach. There are the predators and the preyed-upon, the balance between nature and man, and the conflicts for living space.

There's a special thrill to surfing that many don't bother to experience. Sometimes, on a big wave that's not overly critical, Ricky will glide shoreward and look toward the hills and the palms and then out to the whole panorama of the surf and sea. "You can coast along getting a free ride from nature, the wind blowing in your face. There's the sun. It's not all locked in the tube. It's a beautiful, peaceful thing to do. You're completely free. There are no rules out there, just yourself and the wave."

Ricky is unique in the surfing world, a total man of the sea. His knowledge of the ocean's slowly unraveling secrets deepens his appreciation of this thing of the waves. His scientific background only serves to increase Ricky's deep enjoyment, his sense of fulfillment that the sea and the waves bring. Surfing takes up only a small portion of Ricky's time, his love affair with the sea. Yet when he rides the big ones, in a contest or purely for personal combat, he becomes totally absorbed—and the sea and Ricky are as one.

CHAPTER 7

The Young Men From Florida

Surfing is an art form, in its purist sense.

Bruce Valluzzi

Late one rainy morning in Suite 237, on the second floor of the Royal Hawaiian Hotel, two young surfers from Florida paced restlessly as they watched the tropic storm bend the tall, stately coco palms outside their room. Heavy rain slashed the waves and high-velocity winds sent palm branches crashing to the lush grass below. Waikiki's waves were churned a seething brown and out on the North Shore every spot was blown and rained out. There would be no surfing today. The young men, Bruce Valluzzi and Claude Codgin, cursed the storm. They wanted to be out surfing. It was extremely important to them, they needed the practice. Tomorrow or the next day they would be competing in surfing's Olympics, the Duke Kahanamoku International Championships.

Bruce and Claude had been invited to Hawaii as Florida's representatives in the Duke Contest. "Back East" on the Atlantic Coast a couple of hundred thousand young surfers were hoping their boys would make a showing among the big-wave riders of Hawaii, California, Australia, and Peru. The year before, the one East Coaster invited to the Duke Contest had paddled out, checked the size and strength of Sunset's mighty waves, and wisely paddled in.

95

His defection from the contest, so everyone said, was wise. The Florida towhead who bugged out was being realistic; better to paddle in if you weren't able to handle the heavies. It was better for all concerned; one surfer out of control could injure others. Yes, his decision had been a wise one—but it helped keep alive the conviction that East Coasters couldn't handle big surf, couldn't make the transition from Florida's mini waves to the Hawaiian giants. However, many who had seen the two-man Florida contingent of Bruce and Claude riding out at Sunset Beach knew this was not true.

The boys had wisely come to Hawaii two weeks in advance of the contest to practice. Bruce had ridden Hawaii the year before and had done so well on one day that surfing photographer-dentist Dr. Don James had caught him in a remarkable picture. The photo was so dramatic that it made the cover of *Competition Surfing* magazine. And Claude and Bruce had both been invited to compete in the past world championships in Peru. The boys were almost ready for the Duke Contest—but they desperately wanted one more day of practice.

Bruce and Claude had begun surfing together in Florida five years before, in 1962, when they were in Junior High School. Their hero then was the infamous Murph the Surf, of Star-of-India-stealing fame and other less notorious deals and crimes. But back then Murph was their man, the number one surfer in Florida, the guy who brought modern surfing to the Atlantic Coast. Murph used to make boards at Indiatlantic Beach, and the young kids, top surfers today, hung around their hero as he carved out surfboards. He was on top in those days and the kids watched Murph and imitated his new ways of nose-riding. As Murph toured from Florida to Rhode Island his flashy style on and off a surfboard excited the youngsters of the East Coast and helped start the surfing boom along the Atlantic.

Then Dick Catri came over from Hawaii and helped Murph and the kids dominate every wave spot Florida had to offer. Coco Beach became the East Coast surfing head-quarters. The waves weren't big, but the youngsters were willing, and the kids became deeply involved. Along with

Bruce Valluzzi rides his first big wave at Sunset Beach.
(Dr. Don James)

the pioneering gang, three names soon stood out in the contest circuit: Bruce, Claude, and Gary Propper.

The Florida battle of the surfers involved these three main contestants. Propper was the first of the East Coast's hot young crop, and during his first contest year in '64, he won every surfing meet he entered. From 1964 to 1967, the blond powerhouse from Coco Beach had won over thirty-five first-place trophies and about half that number as runner-up. And right behind on almost every wave were Bruce and Claude. The battle got really hot in '66 and '67, and it carried over from the water to the shore. It was tough on Gary. He had the contest world sewed up for two years. Now younger surfers are beating Gary, and he doesn't give up easily.

The East Coast surf scene also has what Bruce calls the "Lunatic Fringe." These are the "surfies," the guys who are so totally immersed in the sport that they become crashing bores. Some take on wild nicknames and wear far-out clothes. Most of them are not good surfers, but live the wave action so vicariously that there's nothing else in their lives. These are the guys, Bruce claims, who would wind up in a mental hospital if they didn't have surfing. In Florida the lunatic fringe doesn't surf for fun or profit, but for the deep and disturbed need to be recognized. "It's kind of sad," Bruce says, "that so many of the surfie crowd miss the point. You've got to be a person first and a surfer next."

He explained that the trouble with the East Coast surf scene was that it had no heritage. All of a sudden surfing went east and boom! a half a million kids, young and old, were buying boards. In California, at least, guys had been surfing for thirty years before it went big, and the old-timers gave the sport a foundation, some stability. Not so on the Atlantic.

Bruce, Claude, and Gary pushed surfing, giving the sport class and color, and in almost every contest they entered they would be in the top three spots. This kind of rivalry helped draw crowds to the contests, gave surf-magazine editors colorful copy, and provided the photographers with excellent subjects. Above all, their aggressive promotion of the sport sent surfboard sales leaping upward. The board builders the three rode for couldn't have been happier.

Now, four years later, the two glamour kids from Florida sat frustrated in a Honolulu hotel room. They knew that at dawn tomorrow or the next day the Duke Contest director, Fred Van Dyke, would announce at 6 A.M. breakfast that the meet was on. They both knew they would join the other twenty-four contestants in the wild thirty-five-mile ride out to Sunset Beach on Oahu's North Shore.

The Duke Contest, unique in the surfing world, can be held on any one of five preselected days—and at any one of a number of different surfing spots. The idea of a traveling contest permits the selection of the best spot on Oahu on any one day. Depending on wave conditions, the meet could be held at Sunset, Waimea Bay, Makaha, or even the Banzai Pipeline. All but the very gutsiest surfers hoped for Sunset, where waves are usually big but still sufficiently well formed for the hot-doggers to have a chance to show their style. Only a few could really turn on at Waimea Bay, and the left-footed (goofy footers) would have the advantage at the Pipeline, which breaks from the surfer's left.

The rain continued outside Suite 237. The young men from Florida at last relaxed. As lunchtime came and went, they began to reflect on the sport that had brought them so far from Florida to this de-luxe suite in the Royal Hawaiian.

Both Bruce and Claude had involved themselves deeply in the sport. Surfing was paying their way to Hawaii. The Duke Contest officials had given them the room in the Royal Hawaiian and the airplane tickets; and the board builders for whom they rode had provided expense money.

Claude remembered the first time he surfed big waves: "Bruce and I were invited to surf the '65 World Championships held in Peru. It was the first big surf for the both of us.

"We were scared at first, not knowing what to expect. The waves looked huge as they came rolling in out of the morning fog."

"Yeah," Bruce agreed, "and the water was a dark, deep blue and colder than Florida ever gets."

"And there were so many guys there with big-wave reputations. Pomar knew Peru better than anyone else, and Downing and Hemmings and Greg Noll all had years in the big surf. There we were, just seventeen and the first time away from home."

Bruce admitted the first few waves he rode were tough, but then he forced himself to relax after the initial chilling wipe-out and went on to master the waves of Pico Alto, south of Lima. Claude also remembered the waves of Peru. "It was hairy at first and I wasn't good enough then to really appreciate what it took in big waves. The thing that Peru did for me was to increase my interest in big waves. I wanted more and that's why I came to the Islands."

Bruce likes riding big surf. There's nothing better, he feels. But Bruce still doesn't consider himself really experienced in heavy surf. His big day came at Waimea Bay. Bruce had been surfing Sunset and the Pipeline on eight- and ten-foot days when the word spread across the North Shore that Waimea Bay was breaking. Bruce hurried down to Waimea and paddled out with some of the others who had come. He stalled around the outside and watched and waited.

"I'll never forget that first day at Waimea. It was breaking fifteen to twenty feet. I didn't know if I could handle it. Sitting out there I was really impressed by the speed and the power of the waves coming through. Lucky for me it wasn't one of those horrendous days, but it was still big. I guess I rode all right, only took gas once, but that was enough. It's tough unless you're a good swimmer."

Claude hadn't ridden Waimea yet. His baptism in big, fast surf came at the Pipeline, just the day before, his first time at that remarkable spot of tunneling waves. It was fifteen feet. "I went over the falls fast on the first wave, right to the bottom, but gently like, just barely touched the coral. There was more power and speed in those waves than any I've ever handled, more than at Sunset or off Peru."

In the two weeks Claude had been in Hawaii he had ridden all the best spots, except Waimea, which had not showed surf so far that season. He had to gain the confidence that only experience in big surf can bring. "And the great thing about big waves," Claude said, "is that the rest of the guys out there are all cheering for you, and helping when they can. When the old-timers realize you're serious about trying to learn they help and encourage. I guess they've all been through what I was experiencing. It's the guys without real interest, the guys just out there to say they've ridden Sunset or the Pipeline and brag about it, the old-timers don't like."

Both Bruce and Claude admit that surfing has done a great deal for them. Aside from travel and public recognition, they realize surfing has helped them grow, develop an outlook on life, and find a personal philosophy.

In the area of philosophy, Bruce and Claude are as different as they are similar in surfing style and appearance. Both young men are of average height with sandy brown hair and both their bodies show the lean, sleek look of competitive swimmers, with knots on their knees.

Claude, the businessman, looks at surfing as a way of life. He doesn't have any illusions about surfing—it's his thing, his career. Claude works for Con Surfboards as their East Coast representative and during the summer he travels up and down the Atlantic shore from Florida to Maine visiting Con dealers. There's nothing complicated about Codgin and surfing—it's a fun sport, an absorbing business, and the money is good. Surfing has taken him to Puerto Rico, Hawaii, Peru, and all up and down the U.S. seaboard —and all before he was twenty. In the spring of 1968, Claude joined the Petersen Productions film unit on an around-the-world jaunt to try and make a better *Endless Summer*. The trip meant a chance to surf Europe's best spots, which included Biarritz and Portugal's big-wave west and south coasts. He went on to ride waves off Spanish Morocco and then jetted eastward for a week of surfing Hong Kong's Big Wave Bay, which proved true to its name. The filming still continues and Claude will next head for South America.

The best part about his job, he claims, is meeting the people along the way. He feels that surfers are unique, so individualistic that they're almost impossible to fool. Most surfers are realists and demand a straight answer when Claude talks surfboards and surfing.

Girls also go for Claude. That's his major problem when on tour—the traveling surfboard salesman. But this young man has a personal code—no involvement until later, when

This is typical of the fast-breaking waves of the North Shore that challenged
Florida surfers Bruce Valluzzi and Claude Codgin.

(Judy Rohlof, Dixon collection)

he's been most everywhere and ridden all the best waves the world has to offer.

One of the most promising aspects of the surfing life, Claude feels, is that it doesn't have to end. "It's something you can do all your life. It's not like other pro sports—one day you're on the team, the next day you're chopped and will never carry the ball again. There's no such thing as an ex-surfer; perhaps the surfer gets old and plays it careful, but he can still paddle out and ride, and that's what counts. Guys get married and have to get jobs, but once somebody has really surfed and become involved they can't get away from it."

This is how Claude feels it should be. He wants to keep surfing all his life. He realizes that he can't be a contest winner for too many years, but he can still surf and keep experiencing the thrill and satisfaction of a good, fast wave and be involved in something he loves.

The board itself is an object of Claude's love. He looks at each board as a tool for self-expression. The Con Shop builds Claude's boards to his own specifications and unless they meet what he feels is the best in quality, Claude won't allow his name to be used on the board. Every time Claude picks up a new board he checks it carefully to satisfy himself that the lines are true and the workmanship flawless.

Bruce, perhaps because of his background in art, sees surfing as an art form, if also, like Claude, as a way of self-expression. He doesn't regard surfing as a way of life for himself, but as a pre-career that is fun, and that helps him make expenses without grubbing away his younger years at a hateful job. Bruce's college major is art and he paints when at home. He even looks at the waves as an artist will, as something that has three dimensions. Each wave, Bruce feels, has its own individual form and texture and each wave demands a unique response from the surfer. Bruce has also observed that people's personalities are linked to their surfing styles. After a surfer has learned the basic fundamentals, the period of surfing self-expression follows. This is the stage of a surfer's development when he sets his own style.

A surfer who's cool and relaxed, like Hawaii's Jeff Hackman, is the same way on a wave; and the way he handles

the wave is the way he goes through life. Bruce is himself
an example of his own theory. He surfs like a careful artist.
First he looks at the wave, sees its texture and form, then
is slowly inspired. His study of each individual wave before
riding enables him to decide just what technique to use—
and the technique allows him to express himself during the
ride. When he's riding, Bruce savors the taste of the wave
as the salt sea spray is flung back from the board's nose
cutting through the water. He feels the rush of the wave
moving forward and past him and senses the water's tem-
perature. He sees the madly-churning blues and whites and
the dim green-gray of the coral bottom.

But on the wave, Bruce feels, no one is ever right or
wrong. "In surfing you can't judge right or wrong. You
can't criticize. You can only evaluate style and if it's effective or not."

Bruce goes for big waves because he believes there's still
a lot that has yet to be done on a wave and that big-wave
technique is only just beginning. He can make a personal
statement on the wave, expressing his mood. When Bruce
is feeling great and the day is great, he's as aggressive as a
surfer can be. As evening comes and the tropic clouds of
Hawaii take on the dusky pastels of night, his style changes;
it becomes more fluid and graceful—slower and almost
pensive, the way many people respond to sundown.

In the morning, when the chill is still on the water,
Bruce's style changes again—he's more jerky, playful, like a
colt taking his first run across a frosty pasture. And when,
during a contest, another competitor cuts him out of a
wave or causes him to pull out, Bruce becomes the com-
batant and gives back what his adversary gave; this is the
rough and tough part of surfing competition on the East
Coast. In big surf, Bruce observes, "The riders are different,
they don't fool around. The surf's too wild for games." Because the men on the big waves are the best there are,
they don't have to push and shove. That kind of wave be-
havior is for the Florida and East Coast, and for the young
California crowd. "The guys out at Sunset are men, even if
they're only seventeen. And when they ride they act like
men, you know, more serious, mature like. Perhaps because

of the potential danger and all the work it took just to paddle out."

Big-wave surfing, Bruce feels, is total involvement. There's no other way to survive in the heavies but to be committed. "On the East Coast it's different. The only deep involvement comes through the contest route. Half the time you enter a meet and you don't enjoy the waves because they're junky, small and no challenge. On the East Coast there's no way to receive recognition as a surfer unless you win contests, but in Hawaii it's different. Nobody cares if you win or lose a meet, they only care if you're out there and riding well and not getting in the way—kind of like big surf democracy."

Across the hotel room Claude stood by the big window looking out at the sky. The horizon was clearing, patches of blue had begun to show through the storm clouds. Below and out across Waikiki Beach the lines of waves were beginning to show form again. A few people were emerging from the beachfront hotels to walk the wet sand. The first rented boards from George Downing's surfboard empire down at the Waikiki Beach Center were being paddled out by aggressive tourists determined to fill their two weeks in the Islands with every possible experience.

It was midafternoon, there was a chance that the North Shore would be breaking if the storm passed quickly. Bruce and Claude made their decision; they would drive out past the cane and pineapple fields and on to Haleiwa in hopes that the waves were there. This would be their last chance to ride before the contest.

Their guess was right; the surf was holding and they rode till sundown. The next morning Van Dyke decided to hold the contest. The young men from Florida joined the best group of surfers ever assembled and made the wild ride to Sunset Beach. Neither placed or even made the finals, but they both rode their best—aggressively, confidently—as men among the men of the North Shore.

CHAPTER 8

The Aussies

Surfing along the vast Australian coastline has progressed faster and more radically than in any other part of the world. The current world champion and many of today's best surfers are Australians. The names of Nat Young, Bernard "Midget" Farrelly, and Bob McTavish are hero words among the hundreds of thousands of young sun-bronzed and surf-stoked Aussies. Their intense preoccupation with surfing and surf heroes smacks both of nationalism and religious fervor.

The mania for surfing down under has something to do with the country's newness, its position of isolation, and Australia's rapid economic development. Australia has always been sports-minded, probably more so than any other nation. Combine this craze for athletics with almost twelve thousand miles of wave-bashed shoreline, and water sports have just got to develop fast and furiously. And Nat Young, Midget, and McTavish are the waterlogged young men who've given Australian surfing that special flair, that intense drive which has carried their mates forward to become the world's leaders of innovation and aggressiveness in the waves.

Australian surfing, like board-riding in the United States and Hawaii, falls into three separate historical epochs—the long wooden board days, the "Malibu" board days, and the "New Era" of wave-riding. The Malibu board was the name given to the first short balsa-wood and fiberglass-covered

107

surfboards that made the long voyage from Malibu, California, to Australia. The introduction of this short, light, and fast-turning surfboard completely changed the beachgoing life of young Australians—from both a sports and a social point of view.

In the latter part of 1956, just after the Olympics were held down under, the Australian Surf Lifesaving Association invited a group of surfers from California and Hawaii to visit and compete in their lifesaving carnivals. When the Californians stepped off the plane carrying their short funny-looking little boards, their hosts laughed and jeered good-naturedly. The Australian board riders continued chuckling as the Yanks paddled out to surf in the Australian Championships held at Torquay Beach, Victoria.

The smiles and laughs quickly changed to expressions of astonishment as the Californians began *performing* in the waves. The Yanks turned on by riding across the face of the wave, cutting back and making the little boards obey their instant commands. The colorful Americans put on a surfing show that completely dazzled the locals. On those waves were Greg Noll, a big gun in the surfboard building game; Tad Devine, son of the movie actor; and one of the best watermen of the 1950's, Tom Zahn.

The Yank surfers went on tour of the Australian beaches and wherever they rode the beach boys would stand and gape. At Manly Beach, Sydney, the Aussies would wait for hours for one of the Californians to tire and br..ig his board back to shore so they could try the new balsa wonders. A nine-and-a-half-foot, twenty-five-pound revolution had arrived.

When the Americans left for home there were dozens of eager buyers for their boards and very quickly the balsas were being copied in half a dozen home-garage shops. Soon, huge shipments of the light spongy wood were arriving from Ecuador, along with the fiberglass and resin sent across from the States.

Then another shattering import arrived from California —surf movies.

It was just like the California surf boom all over again. The original surf-movie maker, Bud Browne, flew in with his first full-length color film, *The Big Surf*. Australian audiences had never seen the like of the waves Bud's film threw on the movie screens from North Queensland to South Victoria. The young board riders tore the theaters apart. They stomped and cheered and whistled and left the movie houses so stoked that there was no stopping the fastest explosion of sports interest Australia had ever seen. And the style of surfing shown was completely new to most down-under board riders. Youngsters saw the movie over and over again and then went out into the waves and copied what they had viewed so enthusiastically.

Then came *Gidget* in both novel and film version—and just as at Malibu four years before, the Australians flocked to the beaches to make their own surf scene. The scene also involved a non-surfing crowd who lived not for the waves but for the social life. Then came the surfing products, which started a minor economic boom along the beach. Surf-motif T-shirts were the rage and a dozen variations of the surfing fad exploded up and down the long east coast. And as in the U.S., the Aussie surfing craze was used by every commercial huckster to shake a pound sterling from a youngster's pocket. This was the "surfie" period, the time down under when the kids who really went out to ride were looked upon as a tribe of wild teen-age bandits.

One young man of sixteen did it. All it took to change the attitude of adult Australians from negative to reluctant respect was Bernard "Midget" Farrelly's win at the Makaha, Hawaii, International Surfing Championships. His victory made the front page in every major Australian newspaper, as did Bob Pike's win months later in the World Surfing Championships held in Peru.

The rapid growth of surfing's popularity had its effect on Australian institutions such as the famous volunteer life-saving clubs—the kids began defecting. Board riders didn't want to spend long hours drilling in the hot sun for a place on the local club's belt-and-line team.

The Australian lifesaving system is almost paramilitary, and the young men found the freedom and fun of surfing much more to their liking. Today the old lifesaving clubs are slowly dying, doomed out of existence by the surfboard which they had originally promoted as a lifesaving tool. Today the young are not joining the clubs. Beach cities will

soon have to face the awful prospect of employing professional beach guards. Hundreds of jobs will open up for
young men, and most of them will be surfers employed
now because they helped destroy the clubs.

Surfaris then became the thing when gas and money
were on hand. Australian board riders set off first to conquer the waves of their own tremendously long coast. Soon
the beaches immediately north and south of Sydney were
jammed. Next the whole coast from Noosa Head in North
Queensland to Bell's Beach in cold-water Victoria had become log-jammed with surfboards.

The better Australian surfers and those with money
shipped out for new lands and open crowd-free beaches.
Many went to South Africa on the *Southern Cross,* bounded
down the gangplank at Durban like so many board-carrying kangaroos, and started the "New Era" of surfing in
Africa. Others went "home" to England, and the big wet
show began there.

In England, the Australians completely dominated the
surfing scene along Cornwall's Newquay Beach. Rodney
Sumpter, a down-under transplant to the Atlantic, has won
all the European surfing contests for the past three years.
Surfer Sumpter has even ridden the tidal bore up the River
Severn for a continuous distance of six and a half miles.
Rod Sumpter, at twenty-one, has the European surf world
in his pocket. He shows his films, surfs for TV commercials,
travels the world around and owns a store handling surf
products. His Union-Jack-covered surfboard has won him
a shelfful of awards and a fifth place in the 1966 World
Championships.

Australians took their boards from Newquay across the
Irish Sea and there's now an Irish Surf Club with over a
hundred members. The first Irish Surfing Championships
have been held and Kevin Cavey of Bray even went and
entered the World Championships with Rodney—and surfed
to reach the semifinals.

Along California beaches the Australians have been
showing up with their latest "new era" mini boards—fat
and wide shorties that turn on a dime—and, to the horror
of the U.S. surfboard builders, the Australians have begun
to export their fashionable cut-off vee-bottom boards fif-

teen per-cent cheaper than equivalent California models.

Come winter, Hawaiian surfers brace for the arrival of the Australian board riders. They flock to the North Shore of Oahu with their aggressive never-miss-a-wave style. Though Australians have yet to win a Hawaiian big-wave championship (with the exception of Midget Farrelly's Makaha victory), it's not for lack of effort or qualified surfers. So far it's been difficult for the Aussies to translate their unique style to the power and size of the giant Hawaiian surf; but they come closer and closer and the coming season should show the fruit of their development on short boards.

Nat Young's big win at the '66 World Championships inflated Australian surfers' egos beyond the bounds of good taste. A controversy still rages over the merits of Yank and Aussie surfing styles. The Aussies claim they've reached the top spot with their total surf involvement and *Surfer* magazine published an article by Australian John Witzig entitled, "We're Tops Now" that set off a controversy that still runs hot. Surf magazines in both countries have jumped aboard the international conflict and have blown the issue into hundreds of pages of pro-and-con letters-to-the-editor.

The launching of Australia as a world surf power was led by "The Three"—Farrelly, Nat Young, and Bob McTavish. Their respective stories, their contributions, have since been repeated by others along beaches throughout the world, but these three were the ones who started the whole jazzed-up "new era" surf thing moving with such wave-power force.

You have to watch the Australian Three to understand what they are really trying to accomplish in the surf. In a word or two—surfing for Farrelly, Young and McTavish has become total involvement combined with innovation. Their rides, when all works well, are seconds brief, but so completely involved with the wave that surfer and breaker achieve a unity, a oneness with each other. It doesn't matter what brand of swim trunks the three young pros are wearing, what sponsor's board they're riding, or what kind of non-slip coating covers the board's top deck—all the commercialism fades away when they paddle out to surf. And it's the individual battling right in the maw of a fast-

Fred Hemming's radical bottom turn on this Makaha breaker shows the power and grace of one of surfing's most respected big-wave riders.

(P. L. Dixon)

breaking nature-made wave with nothing but his arms and skill and guts that makes for totally involved surfing.

In the days when Australian surfers were completely hooked on anything Yank surf-connected, one very young man stood high above the copycats. This was Midget Far- relly. Midget was outstanding from the very first, so far ahead of his time that it's difficult to understand how he progressed so fast without a hero to imitate. Around 1960, young Farrelly came on the Australian surf scene and in his own quiet, graceful way, went to work and learned in isolation what surfing was all about.

In the beginning, the Aussie surf crew were just out to have fun, earn a local reputation and bask belly-down on the hot sand with their blonde-haired beach girls. But Farrelly saw the possibilities, and worked and worked— and became great. The "Midget" matured and advanced while the others were just bopping around in the shore- break. He was only fifteen, but was already looking ahead to his eventual high priesthood of Australian surfing.

Farrelly, with tousled hair and slim-hipped looks, grew up on the Sydney Beaches. He was born in 1944, the son of a cab driver who gave his skinny son a sense of drive and the love of excitement and travel. Midget was on hand when the Yanks arrived in 1956 with their revolutionary short "Malibu" balsas. When Bernard saw the Americans, "They were doing wonderful things on surfboards, and ever since this sport has been a moving challenge to me as well as a physical test. It's the same for every boy or girl who takes it up."

Midget remembers the day (he was twelve years old) when he found a lost board bobbing around in the shore- break along Sydney's Manly Beach. He told himself he should find the owner, but perhaps he could try it first. He paddled out on the big board, so big he couldn't carry it but had to drag the plank into the water. The first few rides that followed gave him such a thrill, such great elation, that he was forever hooked—bitten deep to the core by the surf bug.

By 1962, Midget had the Australian surfing world for his own. He had never followed or copied, but had innovated on his own. His functional and graceful style has yet to be equaled. Midget began to promote, write, design, and build boards. Many of the young Australians either followed his lead and joined the Midget clique, or turned away and formed anti-Midget groups. Then came the Makaha Championships, and Midget and Dave Jackman were invited to Hawaii to represent Australia along with magazine publisher Bob Evans, who was to help judge. Jackman was also a surf hero, the first to ride successfully the huge Queenscliff "Bombora," a place of high waves that break far from land.

The Australians arrived in Hawaii just two hours before the start of the preliminary heats. They just had time to reach the Makaha shore and a few minutes to paddle and loosen the stiffness of the long plane ride from Sydney. Midget paddled out and went on to win and his broad smile when accepting the trophy betrayed his youth and innocence.

Midget came back from Makaha a much more aggressive surfer, determined to make the sport his life. For some reason Australians resented the avalanche of publicity that swamped Midget. The Australian surf crew, the guys who used to pal with Midget, turned away. They put him through the coals. John Witzig, the top Australian surf editor-writer, nailed Midget to the editorial cross and almost slandered him. It was: "Midget's dead, he's washed-out and old-fashioned, beyond his peak." But Midget remained consistent, true to himself, still the same dynamic surfer. He didn't grow bitter, but kept on surfing well and smiling and coming up with new ideas for better boards.

Now the cycle has come around and Midget is back in the graces of Australians and Witzig is the current low man. Now Witzig comes to Midget for interviews and copy. That's the surf world.

On or off a surfboard Farrelly is smooth, relaxed and competent. During the big beautiful surf that hit Haleiwa on Oahu's North Shore in December, '67, Midget was there and surfing better than ever. It was a true contest, but unofficial and unnoticed except by those in the water. Midget dominated Haleiwa so completely that the North Shore gang went around talking of his rides for days. Midget set the Australian style of surfing for several years, but there were others who were rising and wanting his number one position. Perhaps the biggest and most aggressively-fought surf battle in Australia pitted The Three in a do-or-die clash for supremacy when Nat Young, Bob McTavish and Midget went into the '67 Australian Championships at Bell's Beach.

Bell's Beach lies in the south of Australia, right at the bottom of Victoria where the water's cold and giant swells race north from the Southern Oceans. This Australian National Championship was the first real "new era" contest. The surfers who paddled out into the chilling fifteen-foot surf on their new short boards with the radical v-shaped tails and flexible fins were determined to prove that their new ways would work in big waves.

Into the finals went Nat, Midget, McTavish, and a young newcomer from New South Wales, Peter Drouyn. These top four put on a fantastic surfing display. Nat, so aggressive and confident, ripped into each wave, trying to kill it, and powered his way to first place. Right behind were Drouyn, Farrelly, and McTavish. Midget surfed as gracefully and as beautifully under control as ever, but it was a day for power and Peter Drouyn turned it on.

The judges were troubled. The score was so close between Midget and Peter that when the final tally came in, Midget settled for third by two points and Bob landed in fourth place two points behind. The marvelous performance the Aussies pulled off on their short boards seemed to settle the question of "long v. short, grace v. power" forever. Australian surfing had found its own place, had come of age at Bell's Beach.*

At twenty-five, Midget is the senior member of the top Australian surfing crew. He has given the Australian surf scene more than anyone else. He was followed and imitated and scorned. But now he has found his niche as Australia's number one surf writer, builder of excellent boards, and spokesman for the rational approach to the sport.

Bernard is also cool, collected, and far more mature than most of his contemporaries. He never bothered to hold animosity toward the people who said petty things. When the

---

* During the '68 World Surfing Championships Midget took second place, *one* point behind the winner—Hawaiian Fred Hemmings, Jr.

Bernard "Midget" Farrelley cranks a hard turn at the World Championships, San Diego, California. (Eric Thornberg)

drug issue, the pot and LSD, hit Australia, Midget never went through the dope phase. He remained aloof, quite happy to find his mind expansion out in the water on a fast-curling wave. Five years ago Midget wrote in *The Australian Surfboarder* his basic feelings about the sport: "It is this intense elation that ensnares a board rider, and unless you appreciate this you will never understand surfers. If you want real emotional kicks, this is it."

And then out of Queensland came Bob McTavish, at first only another young beach-bum board-shaper who surfed well. Suddenly this smallish powerhouse was the talk of the surfers. They said:

"McTavish hit Noosa Head on a ten-foot day, ripped the bloody waves apart all day long."

"McTavish, that little bastard, he's too much. Rode Sunset at 16 feet on his 8' 6" Vee-Bottom. Wiped out three times in a row, serves the cocky little bastard right."

"McTavish, he's an intellectual, his mind's waterlogged, though."

"I'd caught about five waves when I dropped in on McTavish—foolish. He swore stunningly at me, causing me to fall off."

"McTavish was responsible for the so-called 'new era' in surfing. I personally think McTavish is the best in the world."

Here's a guy, one of those unique individuals, who stands out in a crowd. He may be just watching and thinking, but his self-contained and relaxed presence just makes itself felt. Picture a very young James Cagney type, muscular upper torso supported by short strong legs and knotted knees; add a sharp nose and strong chin and top him off with sandy blond hair—and you've got a hint of what Bob McTavish looks like.

Bob McTavish missed the World Championships at San Diego. Nat Young says he was the only surfer in the world who could have beaten him. Bob couldn't visit the U.S. at that time—a slight problem involving the American immigration authorities. It seems that in 1963 Bob had an overpowering desire to ride Hawaiian big surf. But he was broke. Being out of cash didn't stop McTavish. With his usual directness he found a freighter bound for Honolulu

Australian "New Wave" founder, Bob McTavish, rides his short board at
Queenscliff, Australia. (Alby Falzon, Dixon collection)

and stowed himself aboard. He reached the Islands, slipped quietly off the ship and thumbed his way to the North Shore All went well. He was the ideal immigrant. Bob was even employed as a house painter between glorious days of surfing Sunset Beach and other North Shore spots.

One day while he was slapping white lead onto a sun-warped termite-ridden beach shack, the immigration people found Bob. Had an enemy passed word of his illegal status to the law? No. The tip came from a young Sydney surfing columnist. The writer just happened to think Bob's free trip to Hawaii would make interesting copy—which it did for the U.S. Immigration people. Now Bob has paid back the shipowners who gave him free passage and the U.S. has forgiven all. Bob has since visited America and surfed the waves of California.

McTavish surfed into Australian competition with real power. He doesn't like competition surfing, but of the four major Australian contests he has entered, the record stands: Queensland Championships, winner twice in a row; second and third in the Australian Championships. But in his favorite size waves—screamingly fast eight- to-ten-footers—he's number one wherever he surfs.

McTavish and most of the current crop of top Australian surfers owe a great deal to a quiet, young, and unpublicized Californian. Their involvement, their skill at playing it close to the curl, the evolution to the short boards, grew in part from the two visits of George Greenough. George, a sort of surfing wizard from Santa Barbara, California, has come up with more creative ideas in surfing and photography than most men could conceive in a lifetime. And George and McTavish together, one creating and the other bringing George's ideas into practice, really sparked the whole Australian surf scene.

Bob McTavish was a nobody when he first came down from North Queensland to Sydney and found a job in a board shop. Nobody knew him nor cared for the cocky little guy. In the Sydney area McTavish developed background, learned the trade of board building, and slowly gathered momentum as he surfed the New South Wales breaks. When Bob felt his apprenticeship was complete he returned to Queensland and the wonderful waves of Noosa

Head. There, among what he calls ". . . the most complex waves of the world's known surfing spots . . ." Bob worked and practiced to master the basic arts of surfing. At Noosa he rode the breaks of Nationals and Tee Tree, learning always more of the way of waves, gaining experience and skill that only weeks and weeks of surfing can bring. Then grinning and innocent George Greenough arrived at the Sydney airport wearing his huge baggy overcoat.

While McTavish fought the waves off Noosa and grew stronger, Greenough fought his way through Australian customs. George had come across the Pacific at the invitation of Bob Cooper and his glowing reports of wonderful uncrowded surf. As he stepped off the plane, with his hydroplane belly board under his arm, the Australians waiting to meet George whispered among themselves, "Out of sight! No! I don't believe it." And the customs people went out of their skulls as George opened his bag and overcoat. From the bag came special Greenough surfboard building tools, miles of still and motion picture film, and several pairs of his faded and worn bathing suits. And when he opened his overcoat, they gasped. Built into the lining of the coat were special pockets designed to hold George's full line of camera gear. His cameras and cases were all handmade, crude but efficient. George pulled all his stuff out, plopped it down on the customs counter, and stood back. After the hassle over duty had been settled, George stepped out of the airport to dazzle the Aussies.

The Aussies couldn't fathom George at first. They were expecting some sort of cool American cat, polished and citified, which George is not. They were also troubled by the fact that George didn't ride a surfboard, but only his radical, self-designed fiberglass belly boards. George went north with his ideas and his belly board and met McTavish up at Alexander Headlands, Queensland.

Up on a hill, in a rustic pink house overlooking the surf, Greenough, McTavish, and a handful of other great Australian surfers settled down to surf and talk seriously. George would expound theory and then hit the water to kick out to the break on his belly board and rip the waves apart. McTavish would watch and figure and then attempt the same on his surfboard. George was the catalyst that blew all the American styles and fads out of Australian minds. George said, "Cool it, forget the crap in the surfing magazines, do it your own way." And McTavish and Nat Young watched and were dazzled by George. McTavish was able to translate to his surfboard what George was trying to demonstrate on the belly board.

Then things started happening. George designed the flexible fin and McTavish went out and proved its worth. Next came the first short boards conceived especially for the Australian surf. This was an enlargement of Greenough's belly board that really ripped. Soon George was coaching the board builders, having them chop off a little here and a little there, and as the boards grew shorter, and fatter, McTavish would paddle out and test.

McTavish had the special ability to assimilate all that George was trying to do, and he succeeded remarkably. The others, like Nat Young, could then watch McTavish and see him doing the Greenough things—and make the transition to their own boards.

North Queensland and Noosa Head have special significance for Bob. It's where it began for him and where he best likes to surf. At Noosa Head there's his favorite break, Nationals. Bob says of this special place, "The waves of Nationals are the best thing I know in surfing. Riding them is second best. What is a National wave? A series of incidents that add, tie up to a tale, a being. One minute a pressure, then a cruise of ease, euphoria, next a calculus, finally, always finally a satisfaction. One pure slice of existence. Being."

Of the surf of Queensland, Australia's warm north coast, Bob says, "There's more surf there than anyplace in the world. I've surfed the north coast for ten years. There's hundreds of spots yet to be ridden. And warm water, it's beautiful. Ten years ago there was nobody there. People are friendly, camping is easy, no cops to bother you, traveling's a joy."

The United States bothered Bob. "You've got 200,000,-000 people. It's amazing. You've so many rules to control them, so many licenses, registration papers, numbers, forms and cards. Australia's starting to get that way. It's a pity."

Surfing is a business for Bob. He acknowledges what it

has done for him. In his board shop he's a businessman, but out in the waves he's having fun first, promoting himself second. In Australia "The industry is still growing. Production is up, but there are more surf shops, more shapers. Quality gets better and better. That's good for the industry. Competition among board builders isn't like in the States. Nobody wants to cut the other builder out. And the shapers are content to carve out five or six boards a week. Nobody's killing themselves."

What is important about the Australian surfing world, Bob feels, is that the people involved are growing up, getting over the ego thing. "Australia's wide open. Surfing politics are in good shape. The clique days are over. There were wars and feuds, too many chiefs and not enough surfers. All this has gone entirely. The numbers of surfers are overwhelming. Surfing is now a very simple thing, you just do it." And McTavish does it better than anyone, except perhaps Nat Young.

Even when Nat was a tiny little kid with huge feet surfing off the Sydney beaches he could do anything on a surfboard. He was awkward, to be sure, but he stuck to his board. He couldn't be knocked off. Nat and the other beach kids started when they were ten and twelve and by the time they were twenty the now-greats had ten years of surfing and contest experience behind them.

Nat stands in the center of the current Yank-Aussie surfing-style controversy. Nat is a world champion and a professional surfer. He's in the surf game for profit and fun, and in that order. Nobody works harder at being and staying number one in Australia. He's probably the most aggressive surfer in the world. Watching Nat surf proves this. He's in movement all the time, always surfing with a "heads up" attitude. As soon as a ride's finished, his board gets whipped around and started back toward the break and Nat's ready for one more wave.

Nat will try anything on a board. In a wave, he experiments and works and works—like McTavish—until the new idea becomes part of his routine of movements, or proves impossible to perform. Bob Cooper, who has watched Nat progress from a skinny Sydney surf Gremmie to number one, observed, "He really wasn't a natural. He is also taller

Nat Young, hanging five, during the United States Surfing Championships
at San Diego, California. He won.

(P. L. Dixon)

than most hot surfers, which is a slight disadvantage, and awkward. I don't see how he did it except through aggressive determination and gut-aching work."

Like a boxer or football quarterback, Nat enters surfing contests with a plan, a preconceived strategy. He studies the competition, knows who's up and whom he must outride, and sizes up the quality of the judges. Judges are important to Nat because he knows he is surfing for points and not for the crowd or himself.

The judging of contests bothers Nat greatly because he defines surfing as an art and art is a form of self-expression, and as Nat says, "How can anybody judge self-expression?" But then contest winning brings favorable publicity and without notoriety the sponsors won't pay and the bathing suit companies won't shell out for endorsements.

Since the days when Midget set Australian surfing styles and Phil Edwards led the California crowd, Nat has tried to be his own man, follow his own thing. Nat reasons that as long as you have someone to follow, how can you possibly lead?

Nat's own thing didn't come easily. While he was developing his remarkably aggressive and radical approach to wave domination, people laughed. In Hawaii, at Makaha '66, they snickered when Nat paddled out on the first really short board to enter big-surf competition. Every waterwise surfer in the Islands warned him that his equipment was wrong for Makaha, but Nat persisted and rode his postage-stamp board anyway. He was learning, developing his own special style and trying to prove it would work in Hawaiian big surf as well as in smaller home waves.

At Makaha, Nat fought the surf in his own terms. The waves were big that warm December day just before Christmas and the competition was extremely tough. The major scene of the wave action was taking place outside the normal break, far outside the famous "Makaha Bowl," a giant break that only shows when swells are extremely large and powerful.

When Nat paddled out at Makaha there was a ripple of excitement among the surfers on the beach, and among those who knew of Nat's strongheaded persistence in ignoring the advice of the experts, the kings of Makaha surf.

Nat paddled furiously straight for the bowl. He tried and tried to master the fast steep-walled waves in his own way. Again and again he would take off and shoot down the wave's face and, as he made the bottom turn, his small board would spin out. Nat would eat surf as his board bounced in with the white water to shore. After half a dozen long swims to retrieve the board, even Nat was exhausted. On the beach, those spectators who knew what he was going through could imagine the inner screams his arms and back made for rest.

As the final heat drew near its conclusion, Nat must have figured out the problem—control. He relaxed, rested just a minute, and then on the next giant wave let his body and board flow as one. And as one they came ripping in together. He had beaten the bowl his own way, but had used up almost all the time remaining in the heat.

Nat didn't paddle back out but decided to remain inside, in the vicious Makaha shorebreak. He would use the remaining minutes really to turn on his own thing, his own style. In the shorebreak, near the judges, in lightning-fast surf that broke almost completely from top to bottom, Nat showed himself. It was an astonishing display of skill and control, brief seconds of glorious performing under horrible conditions. Nat was so tight up inside the break that most watchers didn't understand what he was trying. He dominated the shorebreak as nobody else had before. But the judges' eyes were watching the bowl, seeing only the Hawaiians and the mainland big-wave riders doing their thing, the same thing they had been doing during the past ten contests—riding the heavies like bronze gods of old. It was pretty, beautiful even, but to Nat and others it wasn't involvement. It wasn't pressing to the utmost limits.

Nat didn't even place in the Makaha finals, but he did prove to himself that his way in the surf would work—and to Nat that was the reason to be out there.

Now the Aussies are tops, sure of themselves, and headstrong and aggressive to boot. They have ideal conditions, a wave environment so rich it's likely they will continue to dominate. And so it goes down under until the next phase, the next page is flipped. Whose turn will it be then?

CHAPTER 9

The Wet Jet Set—Economy Class

> There is no turning back the clock on the waves. Just as the roads are doomed to being ever more congested, the edge of the sea is predestined to become an area bristling with boards and their riders.
>
> Peter Viertel

The sleek silver jets of Boeing and Douglas have cut the time barrier across the major oceans of the world. The price of a ticket to any beach on this earth can be saved by most who are willing to work. Surfers have used the fast jets to take them across the time- and distance-barrier to where the waves break clean and free of the crowds that profane their sport. For many surfers it was either give up, or push on and fly to where the water's warm and the waves are open.

Almost every surfer becomes a habitual wave watcher. Whenever a true wave hunter is within sight of any large body of water, he's searching for a potential surfing spot. You can spot every surfer on the jet to Hawaii, even if he's wearing a suit and tie, by the way he peers from the window and down to the sea when the plane leaves or approaches land. And more than one traffic accident has been caused along coast-following roads by a beautiful wave formation diverting a surf hunter's eye from the highway.

All around this sea-encircled world, surfers are pushing outward to seek the better break and the uncrowded wave.

128

The hunt for the perfect wave has led the small band of determined surf seekers to many adventures along dozens of distant and isolated coasts.

The beaches of Ceylon and Singapore, the waves of Brazil and Britain, the surf of El Salvador, Morocco and Fiji, of Guam and the Azores and the Canaries and Japan, have all been discovered by wave hunters on surf safaris.

All are looking for an equal to the Hawaiian waves, that perfect place where the waters are warm and clear and the break holds and holds and you've got it all alone, all to yourself to ride and ride until exhaustion drives you to the beach to rest, to eat and sleep and to wake in the morning and find the waves still there—only bigger—and still your own.

The stories of these wave hunters, the surf pioneers, will never make history books because their searches are for selfish, personal reasons—the surfer's own fulfillment. The wave discoverers may make known their finds, but only to friends and to the limited readership of the surf magazines. Their travels won't produce a surf-tourist boom. Only a few will follow at first because surfing is essentially a low-budget way of life. The older middle and upper classes enjoy their formalized comforts and cocktails after a few hours on the ski slopes or golf links.

Only in Peru and France has surfing taken on the refinements of surf clubs with warm showers and cafes with waiters. Elsewhere after surfing, the board riders huddle for warmth by driftwood fires and wrap themselves in old army blankets. For food they may eat bananas in the tropics, dry peanut-butter sandwiches in North America, and perhaps cold tortillas along Latin American beaches. Most sleep on the sand, a few in hammocks, while the lucky ones along South Africa rest in clay and straw-roofed rondavals for fifty cents a night.

The waves that break along the coasts of this world's major oceans have drawn surfers to many strange beaches. Ed Greevy, once publisher of *Competition Surf* magazine, found excellent waves along the rocky and fog-shrouded shores of Nova Scotia. Far-traveling surf photographer-writer Ron Perrott discovered a tropic paradise of waves out in the middle of the Indian Ocean along the shores of the Seychelles Islands.

Surf cinematographers Greg MacGillivary and Jim Freeman toured the coast of South America and found excellent waves at Playas, Ecuador, and Mike Doyle and an Aussie friend discovered a place of waves at Salinas in the same country. Peru, of course, has been the South American surfing paradise for years, but recently Lima's exploring surfers have added half a dozen new spots to their list. Across the Andes the team of MacGillivary and Freeman surfed at Mar del Plata, Argentina, and then went on to find waves at Punta del Este, Uruguay. Surfers have been riding the breaks off Rio de Janeiro for many years, but recently new spots have opened up along this vast Brazilian coastline. The author and his family and a friend were the first to ride the waves of El Salvador and found that the potential for surf in this smallest of Central American countries could make it another Hawaii.

One of the most fascinating stories of surf discovery was brought to print in the French magazine, *Réalités*. Peter Viertel, the Hollywood film writer, told how the first surf-boards, the *planches du surf*, were brought to Europe. Some years ago Viertel was sent to France to script the film version of Hemingway's *The Sun Also Rises*. At Biarritz, the writer was astonished and absolutely bug-eyed to see set after set of crisp clean surf rolling in from the Bay of Biscay. Viertel, an old Malibu surfer, had his boards air-freighted to France. Soon the writer and a handful of Frenchmen were paddling out to start the European surfing boom. With Mr. Viertel's and *Réalités's* kind permission, here's what happened off Biarritz twelve years ago:

> "How does it work?" they would ask.
> "You lie on the board and the boat pulls you . . ."
> "There is no boat."
> "But what makes the board move?"
> "The waves."
> "The waves? I don't understand."
> "You paddle with your arms," (*ramer* is the French for paddle, I discovered, the same as row) "and once you have enough speed, the waves take over, and you get up and ride the board, steering it with your feet."
> "I see. And how long is the surf?"

"You mean the board. Surf is the English word for breaking waves . . ."

"*Bon.* The board, then?"

"Nine to ten feet. Sometimes even longer, depending on a man's weight and size."

"Aha, I see. *C'est comme le ski nautious.*"

"Not at all."

Those were the conversations of long ago. Now even the most earthbound Frenchman knows that the long plastic sharks on the tops of cars in this part of the world are *planches du surf,* and that they are used for riding the waves that roll gently, and not so gently at times, on to the beaches of the Pays Basque. Occasionally an ignoramus from the Ile de France will still ask, "*C'est un bateau?*" But the same Frenchman might well inquire about the purpose of the stone-walled village *fronton.* For surfing is now almost as solidly established in this, the most southwesterly corner of France, as is the traditional game of ball and basket and hand. Ten, twelve years ago it was different. There were only a few of us riding the waves at that time, or trying to do so at considerable risk to life and limb.

Spurred on by the sporting desires of young Richard Zanuck, who is now a desk-bound studio chief in Hollywood, I had taken the first two surfboards to Biarritz in the early fifties. The waves, we had both realized on an earlier trip (while scouting locations for the filming by 20th Century-Fox of Hemingway's *The Sun Also Rises*), were perfect for the sport that had already gained a solid foothold on the minds and bodies of the youth of California. The water was warm, and although the weather was not as relentlessly sunny as that of Southern California, the conditions were ideal for this, the bravest and most strenuous of all water sports. Young Zanuck was sent home by his father to exert himself in the more troubled waters of the movie industry, leaving the boards and me behind. I found a handful of eager enthusiasts in the neighbourhood, and the craze was launched in France.

The pioneers of French surfing were a mixed lot. There was Joël de Rosnay, an excellent skier and body surfer; André Plumcoque, the athletic proprietor of a ladies' and gents' beauty parlour; Michel Barland, the fearless owner of a machine-tool factory; and a heavily muscled young lad named Rott, who arrived

The author coming in on a Zunzal, El Salvador wave. The local people report surf breaks bigger most of the year around.

(Sali Dixon)

from the Landes region and tried to make a surfboard out of plywood and canvas, a not too successful first experiment.

Each one of us contributed to the birth of this sport. Joël de Rosnay had a natural gift for public relations, and he soon had the mayor of Biarritz as well as the officials of the various French sporting associations interested, although very little was done to facilitate matters with customs and the beach authorities. Rott and Barland became the manufacturers of the now perfected French surfboard, and Plumcoque spurred others on with his example of dogged physical prowess and dedication. I supplied the first *"engins de surf,"* as the stern-faced customs man ordered me to describe them in my official request for an import license.

Surprisingly enough, there were almost no victims involved in these first attempts to walk on water. One unfortunate bather ran out to retrieve a runaway board, only to have *"le surf"* jump up and hit him in the jaw. Teeth went flying on to the moist sand, while I apologized and wrung my hands, thinking that an enormous lawsuit was sure to follow. The man smiled (a less pleasant smile than the one he had come to the beach with that morning) and asked me not to worry, assuring me that the teeth had not been his own in the first place, and that his wife had been after him to get a decent set for years. Soon you could count half a dozen broken noses among the gilded youth of the Côte, but they were considered a small price, gladly paid for all that pleasure. As I was one of the pioneers, my wife and I were accorded free showers and changing privileges by the bathing authorities of Biarritz, and all was well with the world of the summer sun and the sea.

Now the craze is rapidly crescendoing. Americans and Australians and New Zealanders, and Englishmen from Jersey and Cornwall arrive early in the summer now, to camp or inhabit the small hotels of the region. Surf "bunnies" and "gremlins" abound on the more popular beaches of the region, where, stretched out in their bikinis, they lie watching their idols cavort on the waves. There is always somebody who knows how to strum a guitar, and while the tide rolls in, the music of the Beatles and the Rolling Stones lingers on in the warm air, casting off, or so it seems, a vague aroma of suntan oil. To have sun-bleached hair is almost a must

The broken window of a deserted villa frames a surfer at Guethary, France.
(Ron Perrott, Dixon collection)

these days, just as important as having a brightly-colored board strapped to the top of one's Citroën, or a pair of knee-length Hawaiian shorts. But sadly enough for us, the pioneers, there is hardly room to "hang ten," or do a decent "kick out" nowadays, for the waves are so crowded that even a female neophyte is not received with open arms, as she would certainly have been in the fervent fifties, the day the "surf settlers" came to the Bay of Biscay.

There is no turning back the clock on the waves. Just as the roads are doomed to being ever more congested, so the edge of the sea is predestined to become an area bristling with boards and their masters. That is the reason for the sad note in this report. Joël de Rosnay performed his task too well. So perhaps some of us will have to move on, to Spain and Portugal, where the big waves are still a signal for all sane folk to flee the water and remain on land. I suppose the "grand tour" for the youth of the future will soon include an extended visit to this, the birthplace of European surf. And while parents are sweating off their excess weight on the golf course, or losing their francs in the casino, their sons and daughters will while away their hours with the breakers and the gremlins on the beach. Why, you may ask? What is the mysterious hold that this sport has on young people? Why do they all get so permanently hooked? Well, as a young American surfer explained it to me: "It's a free ride . . ." Which is a *raison d'être* for sled and ski and the big boards on which a man can slide across the wave.

Years ago a sporting wag in Malibu scrawled the words "PRAY FOR SURF" in bold letters on the side of a beach house. The next morning another inscription had been painted below the original message. "PRAY FOR SEX" was written there, "YOU CAN SURF ANYTIME!" At this late writing, no such sacrilegious spirit is in evidence here in the Basses-Pyrénées, and the water will grow ever more crowded with young men and women, who are still content to dissipate their strength in the blue and white waves near the shore. More proof that there is no pleasure reserved for the chosen few.*

---

* Viertel, Peter, "Innocents Aboard," *Réalités*, English Edition, No. 204 (November, 1967), 58–59, 102.

Now the French surfing areas along the Bay of Biscay have become crowded during summer when the hordes of young European surfers come for the season. The de Rosnay brothers have moved on to work their way westward to the surf of the Spanish and Portuguese coast. The surfers of the Channel Islands of Guernsey and Jersey join forces in the fall to charter a plane and fly on to the waves of Portugal and even to Agadir on the coast of Spanish Morocco.

The British Isles and Ireland have joined the surfing world and the transplanted Australians have demonstrated to them what sport can be had from the big bad and cold breakers of the Atlantic.

The Australian who really showed the Europeans what high-performance surfing could be like was Rodney Sumpter. At twenty-one, Rod Sumpter has won all the European surfing championships for three years, has traveled from the Irish Sea south to Equatorial Africa, and has ridden the famous tidal bore up the River Severn in Gloucestershire, England—for six and a half miles.

The Australian surfing crew enjoying the relative warmth of a Cornwall summer are members of the down under Wind and Sea Surf Club, escaping their winter, the opposite of England's. Sumpter, as leader of the overseas Australians, dominates every contest he enters, every wave he rides. Rodney has won so many European surf meets that his popularity has suffered. Until somebody comes along to beat him there's not much chance of the local British, French or Irish surfers taking home a trophy.

By law Rodney is really English, being born in Watford in 1947. His family moved to Australia when he was six months old. Rodney grew up along the Sydney beaches, about a hundred yards from the waves of Avalon. At fifteen he won the Australian Junior Championships. That winter Rodney returned to England, helped start English surfing, and then sailed for the United States to compete in the World Titles. He ended up in fifth place. His Union-Jack-covered surfboard was the most photographed object in the contest.

Sumpter has endured and become a pro surfer. Besides the contest route, Rodney makes surfing films, distributes

Former European surfing champion Rodney Sumpter won the Cornish Open Championships here at Porthtown Beach, Cornwall, England.

(Dixon collection)

his own and other movies around Europe and South Africa, and of course endorses surf products.

At twenty-one, Rodney has developed into an effective, self-possessed young businessman, having a good time with his life. He has passed beyond the surfing-mystique stage. He surfs to win because winning brings publicity and publicity brings audiences to his films and buyers for his sponsors' products. He's serious about his surfing, and its training all year around, even when winter settles over Newquay Beach, Cornwall, and the snows blow down from the north.

There are trips, however, just for the sake of adventure and to ride where others have not gone before. A recent journey took Sumpter and his friend Ian Harewood from Jersey to Africa and the steamy waves of Cotonou, Da-homey—a tiny former French Colony on the Atlantic Coast. The waves were great. There was not a single surfer for thousands of miles and the wonderful warmth of equatorial waters chased away the chill of England. Sumpter and Harewood enjoyed the paradise of African waves but they had to return. It was time for Rodney to try riding the Severn Bore again.

He had attempted the tidal wave once before, but the wave had come too quickly, spilled over the small human, and rushed on. Rodney had a better plan now. He was sure it could be done.

The Severn Bore is a single wave that sweeps up the Severn River during spring and fall high tides. As it enters the wide river mouth rushing northward, the wave is only a few inches high. Farther along the Severn, the banks narrow and the wave rises and grows until a perfectly shaped and ridable wall of water forms. The clearly visible wave runs upriver for twenty-six miles from Sharpness to Gloucester at twelve miles per hour. For roughly ten of these twenty-six miles the tidal-bore wave forms a clean shoulder to ride on—probably the longest makable wave in the world. In 1967 Rod Sumpter rode the Severn Bore six and a half miles. Here's how he tells it:

I have explored the Severn many times and believe it is one of the most unusual and ideal surfing spots in the world. From a surfer's point of view, the difficulties are to know where and how far from the bank the wave will break, so as not to miss it or go over the falls. I found that sticking close to the bank before the wave comes, and then paddling over to midstream depending on the shoulder, was the best. Also by being close to the bank there is less likelihood of being carried downstream against your will by the out-going river and it is easier to have a line-up point. The river is dirty and full length wet suit is advisable for protection against sticks, logs, and the cold water. The occasional rat or dead sheep may float by, but not to worry, I can assure you of one of the most perfect and exciting rides in the world.

I first heard about the Severn Bore from surfers in Cornwall and Bob Head of Australia was the first to ride it in 1964 for a hundred yards. I would not say that the bore is the ultimate for all surfers but for a sufficiently experienced surfer it is a six-mile ride of hollow tubes peeling off from the banks with perfect sections. It is a reef, point and beach break wave rolled into one. It is a difficult wave to ride and without experience a surfer is likely to miss it and be disappointed.

I first rode the Bore in February 1967 at Minsterworth for two hundred yards. After heavy rains the wave was big but choppy. Three members of a British pop group, the Fenmen, paddled out with me but having very little experience, missed the wave. In October 1967 I successfully rode it for six and a half miles from Broadoak to Longney. The main problem on the long ride was to try and judge on which side of the river the wave would keep breaking and which side would fade out or just slam up against the bank.

I took off at Broadoak, where the banks are one-quarter mile apart, on a small but very strong wave. This part of the river is very shallow and my fin rubbed the sand. Also it was impossible to drop to the bottom or ride directly parallel across the long wall. The river flowing out towards me made it very difficult to beat sections as I could only semi-angle across. The first bend came a mile down and was horsehoe shaped. I was on the inside of the bend but the river was narrowing and I found myself being angled towards the outside bend with the crest fading on the inside. The problem was to corner across the on-coming bank without coming off the back of the wave. I found myself riding about two feet from the bank with mud and foam exploding outwards. This happened on nearly all the bends over the six miles. Three miles further down, the river widened a bit and I was approaching sand banks in midstream with tree trunks and logs, dismantled by a previous bore, marooned on them.

I had to decide on which side of the sand banks the wave would continue to break because it is unlikely to do so on both. I correctly chose the lefthand side and thought I was lucky until I noticed the bank ahead jutting out at right angles. It was too late to change sides so I faded as far out on the shoulder as possible and was able to miss the bank but the inside section slammed against the bank and the muddy, swirling backwash blasted me off the wave.

I had no idea where I was and there was no sign of civilization so I tramped through fields in my full length green wet suit until I found a cottage. A little old lady answered the door and for a moment I think she thought the Martians had landed! I explained I had ridden the bore and she told me I was at Longney on the opposite side of the river to Broadoak. She then directed me to the main road. It was my most memorable ride and one I won't forget.

Anyone interested in repeating Rod Sumpter's remarkable ride can write for a Severn River Bore Timetable from Severn River Authority, 55 Brunswick Road, Gloucester, England. Here's an ideal spot for long lefts and rights under trees, over fields, around drowned sheep, and through bushes!

The jet set surf seeker need not be the typical young hero with a smile on his face and not a care or serious thought in his head. Surfing has matured and mature young individuals are staying with the sport as professionals. Today the profession of "surfer" can be as respectable a way of life as that led by any other professional athlete. Bob Cooper, the bearded board builder-designer of California and Australia, fits easily into the classification surfer-professional. If board builders had guilds or unions Bob would be rated as a master designer-shaper. Bob, with his flowing beard and long reedy frame, is a well-traveled innovator

Bob Cooper—beard, wet suit, and all—rides the fast, curling waves of Malibu. The Cooper-designed and -shaped board is just an inch over eight feet. (P. L. Dixon)

and was largely responsible for bringing the down under surf scene up to its current level of intense high pitch.

Like so many of today's totally committed surfers, Bob began his wet way of life body-surfing the Santa Monica beach breaks. In the days when any kid in Los Angeles could take a streetcar to the beach for a dime, Bob was a regular passenger—after school, weekends, holidays and all summer long. Soon he graduated from body to board and joined the surfers at Malibu and Palos Verdes Cove. His first stand up ride came at Malibu, "A halfhearted try for a three-foot wave. I caught the wave but didn't know what to do next. Suddenly Mrs. Dave Rochlen rode up behind me and said quietly, 'Now stand up, Bob,' and I did."

Then came the age for Bob when a kid in California had to have a car to reach Malibu and carry his old board. Next came the time when his father said, "Work or school, which is it going to be?" College began at Brigham Young University, Utah. Bob drove away from the sea and off to Provo in his '41 Cadillac limousine with two surfboards roped to the top. "The locals really blew it when we drove into Provo. I'd had my beard for about a year then and the hair was plentiful. A very colorful package arrived in Utah." To keep in shape for the next summer of waves Bob paddled against the currents in the Utah irrigation ditches.

During summer there were the waves, the beach and the lazy afternoons at Malibu. But even a bearded poetic surfer needs change for gasoline to keep the black limousine rolling, and a job had to be found.

A favorite hangout for Bob and other young surfers with a liking for the building side of surfing was the Velzy-Jacobs surfboard shop. The scene was typical of the first board builders of California. The shop was an abandoned building nestled among the creaking old oil wells of Venice, California. There, under the rusting derricks, some of the best of the late balsa and early fiberglass boards were built. Hap Jacobs liked the intensely curious Cooper and offered him a job as a board sander. Coop took the position and went to work in an atmosphere scented with raw crude oil, balsa shavings, and the romantic talk of the early surfers.

Bob Cooper, one of surfing's most respected professionals.
(P. L. Dixon)

Hap was the ideal boss. He would always understand when his help was late—the surf was up and they had to take just one more ride. "It was great at Hap's place. I lived in the back room, surfed before and after work, starved, itched and met the best of the early group. I really dug it." Bob continued working when school started again— he just couldn't bring himself to leave what he loved so much. The work was hard but Bob managed to save enough for his first jet trip to Hawaii. He had hopes of appearing in Bruce Brown's first, "Slippery When Wet."

Bob didn't become a surfing movie star, though he did appear in several sequences. Hawaii, during the late '50's, held a deep fascination for Bob. He rode the big surf and enjoyed the life of the North Shore. "I really became excited over the exotic island life. It was starve and scrape to keep alive, but the scene was fresh and real then." Then came a telegram from the National Guard calling him to duty and when that was over it was job-hunting again—but the surf shops didn't need help. They were suffering pangs of converting from balsa to plastic. However, the sander who had replaced Bob also came down with North Shore fever and took off for Hawaii. Bob got his old job back and stayed just long enough to bank sufficient money for a return to the Islands—and the cycle began again.

Surfboard builders at that stage of their business development were a free-swimming lot. Nobody cared seriously about making pots full of money. Building boards wasn't a business, but rather a way of life to support themselves when the waves were flat. During this period Bob worked in shop after shop, always learning more about the very individual art of shaping good surfboards. As long as there were boards to build a place could be found to sleep in the back room. When the rent's free it's possible to save, and free rent helped Bob buy his first plane ticket to Australia.

Bob left for down under in the summer of 1959 carrying a sample of his own-designed A-Symmetrical board —his nine-foot ten-inch sample—to prove the quality of his work. "I'd finally done it. Only a handful of Yank surfers had been to Australia, and none of them had stayed long enough to really find anything. It was true surf pioneering."

As the long Australian coast hove into view and the plane began its approach to Sydney, Bob looked down to where he would meet his future wife and at the wonderful waves that would call him back twice more. "There was that beautiful crescent-shaped bay of Bondi with water so clear you could see bottom from five thousand feet. Surf was breaking everywhere. I liked it even before we landed."

Within hours Cooper was at the beach and looking across the water and at Australian surfers in action. "My first time out was at Freshwater, a beautiful little bay lined with tall surrounding cliffs. There were only a few blokes out. I put on my wet suit with the red underarm trim, with my purple trunks, and paddled out on my white board to join them—with my red beard. They didn't know what was coming at them. It's a wonder they didn't drown me right there and then."

Bob's stay in Australia hooked him for the life down under. If the telegram telling him that his parents' home had burned down and they needed him hadn't arrived, Bob would have stayed. He returned, went to work shaping, and helping his folks. When the emergency was over Bob moved from Santa Monica to Santa Barbara and a job at Rennie Yater's shop. Rennie had the good luck to find a house right on the beach at Rincon and took Bob in.

The next trip to Australia came after a year of living right on wonderful-wave Rincon Beach. Even the marvelous waves of his "front yard" couldn't hold Cooper back. The waves of Australia and the girl he'd fallen for down under were too compelling. It took several hundred boards' worth of sanding before he had the money for his ticket. But the account grew and Bob had enough cash to return to his two loves. "I bailed out of that Rincon dream pad and onto a Pan Am 707 for Australia. I arrived and she was lovely, but didn't love me. So, brokenhearted and only planning to stay a few months I thought I'd have a better look at Australia's waves. After all, what better consolation for a broken romance?"

Up north in Queensland, Hayden Kenny took a close look at Bob's board and put him to work in his shop. The business was quite small then. Kenny turned out only three boards a week, just enough to keep two surfers alive. "It was small time then, but the Australian surfing thing had just started to boom and soon guys' were surfing everywhere."

Board production grew and grew. Kenny's shop expanded and soon the two men were working five days a week. Bob needed help and inspiration and invited George Greenough of Santa Barbara to fly over and work with them. George was soon followed by Bob McTavish and the revolution slowly began. "Greenough had the place in the palm of his hands in no time. Between McTavish, Greenough, Kenny and myself we had the nucleus of what started the New Era thing in Australia. Even to this day every time Greenough goes to Australia surfing mushrooms again. He really pushes his ideas down their throats. The Aussies dig George and he likes them. It works for both."

The bearded man's romantic problems didn't die even with constant work and surfing. Bob decided he'd better bug out or go daft so he headed across the Tasman Sea for New Zealand and another job in a surf shop. "New Zealand was a disappointment. I was on a bummer most of the time. Fortunately I went on a heavy Yoga trip and really got into it. This pulled me through. I found a master who gave me private instruction. The results that I felt from Yoga led me to the idea there had to be a reason for life."

The Indian and Eastern philosophies didn't fit in with the logic Bob wanted out of life. He found it in the teachings of the Church of Jesus Christ of the Latter Day Saints. His Mormon faith grew and Bob found direction from this Christian body of teachings.

It seems strange to find a religious person in the surfing world; the two don't appear compatible at first. But Bob, being the strong individual he is, could make the two ways of life mix and work. As a first-class craftsman he would build the best boards his brain and hands were capable of constructing. He would ride these boards and glory in the sun and waves and the fast pace of surfing. There was no need to worry about anything else. For Bob, religion and surfing the waves from the oceans mix well.

He admits his religious kick has offended surfing friends in the past. "But now I think I've outgrown the ego trip that is so much a part of surfing your way to the top. I've found direct rewards in my surfing ability and attitude through concentrating and trying to know the laws of life on this earth."

The casual visitor to a hot-surfing spot would guess Bob was just another one of California's hippies, but the surfers who know Cooper realize this slightly outlandish-appearing man is one of their own and one of the best ever to ride a wave. And the Australians who befriended Coop in the past are waiting for his return. Bob's going back soon. He and his Australian wife, Willie, are returning to Queensland and he hopes this will be his final jet trip. Bob Cooper plans to open a surfer hotel where the water's warm and the waves roll in fast, tall, and powerful.

Surfers jetting off to Australia in the next few years might just look for Bob's place along the beach in Queensland. If he's not behind the desk, which is most likely, you'll find him cutting up the waves of Noosa Head or Nationals —his red beard dripping beads of warm Pacific spray and his board locked so tightly in the curl it's just got to be Cooper because nobody else surfs quite his way.

CHAPTER 10

The Competitors

Surfing is my life and I care enough about life and
surfing to spend a lot of time thinking about both.
That's the professional part of it.

Corky Carroll

When Corky Carroll walked past the judges carrying his
red crash helmet under his arm, he gave them a flashy
smile. Several hundred girls jammed among the spectators
at Huntington Beach waved and cheered the young hero.
The electricity he carried with him bothered the other
board riders going out to compete with Corky. It would
be hard to outsurf that much popular acclaim; they were
in trouble before the first wave rolled through.

Across the Pacific on the North Shore of Oahu, young
Jeff Hackman and Jock Sutherland created just as much
excitement as they walked down the beach to paddle out to
Sunset's mighty waves. These two, still in their teens, were
crowd pleasers and the TV cameras zoomed in for a
close-up of the pair.

At Punta Rocas, Peru, Felipe Pomar jogged down the
steep path to enter the Peruvian Championships. The young
Latin ladies were impressed. Here was one of their own
on his way to winning. The cameras zoomed in on Felipe.

Australians found another surfing hero in young Keith
Paul who won their 1968 national championships, taking
the crown away from Nat Young, the bad boy of Australian surfing. Bernard "Midget" Farrelly, the old pro, came

out of semi-isolation and picked up third place, to the immense pleasure of the huge crowds.

These young men and a few others are today's surf heroes, the competitors. Their deeds in the waves and on the beach give surfing a special flair and a sense of combat without blood.

Along all the coasts where surfers do their thing a small group has emerged to lead the competitive surfing parade. Surf contests, in big and small waves, have done more to excite the public and promote surfing than anything else in recent years. The competitors took off and went running when the beach-bunny, surf-movie business collapsed and the last page of *Gidget* flipped closed.

The big contests in Hawaii, on both coasts of the mainland, in Australia and elsewhere, draw the TV cameras, the photographers, the magazine writers, and of course the sponsors who pay the expenses of the board riders.

Today there are half a dozen different classifications of champs, carrying a variety of crowns and titles. Fred Hemmings reigns as the current world champion. Corky Carroll holds both the old USSA and current U.S. Championship crowns. To add to the confusion, the current Makaha International Surfing Championship winner is Joey Cabell. Then there's the last big-wave Duke Kahanamoku contest king, Jock Sutherland. In other words, there's really no number one and nobody is really the best surfer in the world.

Everyone would agree that each surfer can only be judged best for an individual contest on one certain day. At Sunset Beach, Jock was best. At Makaha, Joey came through on top. At Huntington, Corky couldn't do wrong.

The competitors are out there in growing numbers wearing their colored jerseys—and at Huntington Beach their plastic crash helmets—for gamesmanship, fun and profit. In surfing there are no divisions between pro and amateur. That will come later when surfing becomes an Olympic sport.

The competitors, the flashy young cats with all that flair and crowd-pleasing pizzazz, are the actors of the waves. When a contest surfer begins winning he has learned three skills perfectly—to impress the judges, please the crowd, and to master the waves at the contest site for that one day and hour. A classic example was Ricky Grigg's win at the 1966 Duke Contest. He won because of his unique ability to gauge wave-behavior, which kept him so locked in the curl most of the day that the judges and audience were jazzed silly by his showy style. He knew his waves so well, even better than old-timers like George Downing and Hemmings, that he never missed a good one or lost a minute swimming after his board. Everyone there with any surf sense knew the judges would give it to Ricky because he was good and he surfed to impress the officials.

Ricky likes to win. It's good for his ego and image. His win was also pleasing for Jantzen Clothes, who keep Ricky on a retainer to model their sportswear—along with Corky Carroll.

Corky also comes over beautifully on television; he's a young master with the smile and surf talk. These two are pro competitors. They have to be good in front of the cameras and crowds and judges or they don't win. Both are excellent surfers and colorful individuals. They know they'll never get rich from surfing, but a win pays the way and helps propel them to distant shores for a chance to ride more waves. And that's what surfing happens to be all about.

Very few competitors actually enjoy surfing in meets. But the contests are their routes to surfing's rewards. All through the summer in California and along the Atlantic Coast the competitors follow the contests to build up points to establish their overall rating. The only positive aspect of the actual contest for the surfer is the chance to ride his best in a heat with only four others of equal ability.

The much-publicized and televised Malibu invitational contest is one of the most popular among competitors. It's about the only chance any of them have nowadays to ride Malibu free from crowds.

Contests are currently held by the hundreds every summer along U.S. beaches, while Australia and New Zealand go buggy with their regional and national surf meets. South Africa and Peru have their own champion-

The Huntington Beach pier pilings lure many competitive surfers, and some even make it through unscathed. (P. L. Dixon)

ships, as does France. Cold-water England and even Ireland are in the contest circuit.

The big competitive balloon didn't just happen. Surfing contests are as old as the time two surfers first raced each other across a spilling breaker to a sandy beach in ancient Polynesia.

Captain Cook, the first European to witness surfing, tells us in his log that the Hawaiian surfers of the 1770's were fiercely competitive. For the Hawaiians, surfing was a form of gambling. Contests were an everyday part of surfing and huge bets were frequently placed. One story tells of Umi, the son of a chief, so stoked with his wave ability that he wagered his life against four large outrigger canoes (worth about six thousand dollars each today) in a contest. The youth won and paddled off four canoes richer.

During the missionary era in Hawaii gambling was prohibited, putting a stop to competitive surfing. However, in the early 1900's, surfing was born anew and contests started again. By this time betting was not the primary reason for surfing. It was man against man on two separate waves. In the early twenties, when the Outrigger and similar surf-paddling clubs appeared, organized surfing meets began again. The first contest held in California took place in 1927 at the since-destroyed Balboa jetty. Even in those days surfing contests drew quite a following. One eyewitness told how huge crowds gathered on the beach. There were prizes and the roads leading to the jetty were lined with Model-T Fords. Guess who won? Duke Kahanamoku took first and his brother Dan came in second.

The next year Tom Blake won the jetty contest. In those days a surfing contest consisted of a long paddle from the beach, out around a buoy, and if a wave happened to come along, the surfers riding in. In 1928 Tom Blake took two boards with him—his regular long paddle board and, strapped to the top, another, a true surfboard. When Tom rounded the buoy and reached the surfline, he abandoned his paddleboard, switched to the smaller surfboard, and easily picked up a wave to race in and win.

In the world of surfing the names of the competitors have become as commonplace as the names of baseball players to inland Americans. Over the years a few surfers have become known nationally through sales organizations, their promotion of surf products, *and* some facet of their personality that drives them to excel in a very difficult game. A few stories about those who survive the grind and stay in the contest race provide an insight into what the competitive surfer faces.

Over the years, Mickey Dora and Mickey Munoz have come to stand apart like the North and South Poles of surfing. Dora, colorful and controversial, represents the old hard corps of surfers who stayed aloof from society and didn't give a damn who got in their way. Munoz, on the other hand, best represents the next era that came along—the good competitor-sportsman surfer to whom "image" was important. Munoz, one of the early competitors, still hits the contest trail in summer.

The others of Munoz's period have dropped out of contests. Names popular a few years back, like Cole, Rusty Miller, Lance Carson and others, are not seen on contest rosters. Others hang on and still manage to win. People like George Downing, Pete Peterson, Dewey Weber, and Mike Doyle still continue to place in contests and their names appear over and over again in the popularity polls conducted by the surf magazines.

Two young surfers of today best represent both the popular and highly-promoted contest surfer and the still-competing old guard of the surfing world. Corky Carroll stands as the number one surf hero today and Skip Fry as the best of the veterans of ten years' surfing competition.

Corky Carroll usually stands loose, relaxed, peering out —sometimes with a grin and sometimes critically—at the world of surfing beneath him. Right now Corky stands on top of the surfing heap, winner of many big contests and voted the number one surfer of 1968.

It wasn't always that way. It didn't come easy.

Carroll started out like a million other young Southern Californians. He was first a gremmie with a big heavy surfboard, an iron cross, and a lot of enthusiasm. He carried himself down to the ocean daily, pushed out and went surfing.

Once in the waves, Corky began to separate himself from the mass of other skinny surfers scrambling for the next

wave. Corky had more than ability. He had intense determination. His skill and compelling drive, linked with his
likable personality, forged themselves into a champion.

"I really don't know what it was that kept driving me,
what to put my finger on to try and explain what pushed
me. It didn't come easy at first, pushing out of the crowd
was the hardest thing I've ever had to do. I remember the
first contest, Huntington back in 1959. I was nervous.
There were thousands of faces staring at me. The loud-
speaker blurted out my heat. I grabbed my board and
paddled out. I got creamed in a big one and lost in the
prelims—I was in a daze for weeks after."

Corky tried again the next year and the next. "It was the
same thing in 1960 at Huntington, but after that, in 1961,
I began to change. I changed my attitude, my thinking
and my surfing style. I was getting older and better able to
deal with the phenomenon of competition.

"The '61 San Clemente Contest marked the beginning
of the change for me. It was a typical summer contest,
small surf, but I won and went on a full ego-trip over it.
I discovered that I really liked to win."

San Clemente was good for Corky and the next year
made history—he won again. And again the year after
that. He kept on winning up and down the California coast.
After the San Clemente contest, Corky went over to the
Islands and took a second at Kuhio. The Hawaiian contest
was another major step. "In the Islands that summer I
discovered another thing I could excel at, paddling. I
paddled my tail off in three contests that year and won
them all."

His ability to paddle well demonstrated to Corky that
he had the strength for big-time surfing competition. Later
that fall of 1963, he entered the Huntington Contest as a
paddler and as a surfer. In the Boys' Division he performed
fantastically in the mushy, misshapen surf, dominating the
waves and beating all the others. After surfing to win, he
went on to paddling, beating the older powerhouses like
Bob Moore, Rusty Miller and Butch Van Artsdalen.

Corky was launched, well on his way.

He began working for Hobie Surfboards, collaborating
with Phil Edwards on surfboard design and coming into

Corky Carroll, toes on the nose, competes in the first Oregon Surfing
Championships at Otter Rock. (P. L. Dixon)

contact with the world of surfing on an international level:

"In 1963 I was nineteenth on the *Surfer* magazine poll, but by '64 I had jumped to sixth—plus winning several awards from civic groups and a first place on the old *Surfing Illustrated* "Juniors" poll.

"I was gaining confidence with each experience, and entering contests accumulates that kind of experience fast. You learn to assess people, judges, waves, and a thousand other things in the brief time allotted for your heat.

"Probably the thing that counts most is confidence. It's almost the whole thing in winning a contest. Next comes the contest spot. You have to have detailed knowledge of a spot, know the bottom like your home break if you expect to win."

Corky Carroll, a tactician, has carefully drawn charts of the many spots he surfs, or plans to surf. He has to know. This is his business. He is a professional.

"Surfing is my life, and I care enough about both my life and surfing to spend a lot of time thinking about it, planning what I want to do. That's the professional part of it."

But Corky Carroll, the number one surfer, the super-competitor, the aggressive, self-assured figure who dominates the world of surfing with his ideas and endeavors, is not a simple person. Like many who rise to the top, and then maintain ascendancy, he has other facets to his personality that are seldom seen.

"I thrive on excitement. That is probably one of the—what would you call it?—motivating factors? Excitement is one of the greatest pleasures afforded to man. High speed, thrilling danger, and adrenalin pumping like hell. I am in a position to achieve—and I'm young enough to appreciate—the sensation. Speed, out of control, guts up thrilling feat . . .

"Life is fast. Why not live it that way?"

Carroll keeps a journal, a small spiral-top notebook filled with carefully printed pages, headed with a date and a roman numeral beside each paragraph. Alone and reflective, he writes down feelings, sometimes illustrating the thoughts with a small line drawing or a scene colored to match the mood.

On top of the surfer's world, secure, and alone with a sunset one evening, he wrote:

> *Times are good now and I am peacefully flowing along with life, smiling as much as possible. Freedom of movement and personal expression through psychological and physical activity and motion are blending themselves. At times a strong wave of accomplishment sweeps over me. Yet that urge is still there, to reach out, to move on, to gain ground on life . . . and to explore myself further. What lies beyond the sunsets and inside those yellow clouds that hang so happily over the ocean? Look up, look down, look around at your empire, your earth, do you see me.*

And not long after that, a line drawing of a surfer on a wave, and the lip of the wave reads:

> *Excitement is nature's way of flipping out—move around—groove in on excitement!*

From the pensive to the elated—so elated that there isn't time to write, only to express in quick images his feelings . . . Carroll moves swiftly on a wave of excitement, committed to a way of life he has created with his mind and body.

The growing excitement of surfing is his own self-made world. Corky maintains it with equal doses of surf, sun, and emotion generated by hard work that pays off. Surfing pays off for Corky, in material success, in fulfillment—but not always in equal balance and often not immediate.

The contest surfer doesn't always have it easy. Corky's win at the Oregon State Championships wasn't easy at all. Even though the type of competition he encountered wasn't up to California standards, the surfing was rough. Corky had to work hard to overcome the very chilling Oregon water and learn the break which the locals had surfed hundreds of times.

In Oregon, Corky surfed himself numb with cold and exhaustion. He had one day to practice before the meet. It was his drive and determination to overcome the cold and the strange area that made his victory possible. No surfer, no matter how good, could have beaten the Oregon gang on their own waves without making a tremendous effort to overcome the cold. When the contest day ended, Corky was so numbed he couldn't climb the long flight of steps to his car—it took two hours before a roaring beach fire to thaw him out.

The way Corky describes surfing shows how much he thinks about the sport. He has that sense of poetic articulation that is the mark of many reflective surfers who are close to and totally committed to the wave.

"Motion—that's surfing—beginning slowly and accelerating with sweeping grace. Grooving into constant pressure, rolling, moving on smoothly and all is caught and suspended. O.K. Now, if you're satisfied that all is well the action can begin again—and this time you lose yourself in a pattern and tempo, then it's rhythmic and together with the waves. You've evolved symmetric beauty. It's been your move."

Competition for Corky is the dog that bites his ankles, forcing him to compete over and over again. The surf-meet circuit turns many surfers off. They'd rather do their wave-riding in isolation. Carroll, now age twenty, doesn't feel that way:

"Competition fills a large part of my bag. My thing is surfing, and contests are an important part of surfing. It's been this way for ten years now and will continue into the future. It doesn't matter if some of the surf stars like it or not because that's the way it is. We wouldn't have today's level of performance without contests; and whatever their shortcomings, and I'll agree there are plenty, they still promote, upgrade and help surfing—and they do it so the public can view what this surfing thing is all about. They are important. They've made me—that's all I can say."

In Peru during the big '67 contest, Corky proved that he's the toughest of the young competitive riders. A case of extreme food poisoning laid him up in the Lima Hospital. He'd come a long way to surf and on the day of the contest the doctors had forbidden him to leave the hospital. The American couldn't stand not being in the water. He found his clothes, quietly left the hospital and, still weak and dizzy, caught a taxi and arrived just before his heat. Like a legend and a modern surf hero he paddled out and won the contest.

What about the future for a guy who has come so far so fast?

"Right now I've got a chance to visit Europe and surf there. I'll be staying for awhile, and though I'll miss a few contests I'll learn a lot by traveling. That's important at this point."

In Europe Corky will rendezvous with surf-film makers Greg MacGillivary and Jim Freeman. Somewhere along the coast of France they'll film Corky ripping apart the great waves that roll into the Bay of Biscay.

"I've been to Peru, the Islands many times, Puerto Rico, up and down Mexico and all over the USA, always competing. I'm not planning to compete in Europe—unless there just happens to be a contest and I'm there."

A handful of surfing names go back five years, a smaller number ten, and then there are those few unique individuals in their forties and fifties who still compete, and thus remain in the surfing public's eye.

To endure successfully in the surfing world, to stay near or on the top, is somewhat like a prehistoric animal surviving the many changes that the world has undergone since caveman times.

Changes in the surfing world happen in days, sometimes even overnight—and the process of evolution, natural selection, that insures the survival of the fittest holds true for most surfers.

Skip Frye is one of those special people who have survived surfing's evolution. He came on the competitive scene early and succeeded in developing an amazing bag of surf-survival tricks that worked well for him in hundreds of contests. In other words, Skip is extremely adaptable and has survived. Currently he's ranked number two in the *Surfer* magazine poll.

At twenty-six, Skip Frye can look back on better than ten years of contest surfing. He spanned the last of the balsa era, went on to ride foam and fiberglass, survived the long board period and the nose-riding craze, and is now deeply involved in the "creative era" of surfing.

It wasn't always easy for Skip. There were times when

the almost white-blond surfer with the sun-eroded face felt the pressure was becoming too much. The constant contest tension nearly produced ulcers and Skip rebelled, dropping out of the surf scene. His protest took the direction of the far-out life bag that succeeded in making him more notorious than famous. But Frye isn't the kind of person who worries about what others think and say. He doesn't regret his past. Rather, he looks forward to his future and the future of surfing. In effect he's like the prodigal son returned.

As the contest season started along Southern California, there were the usual rumors of who was in and who out. The whispers grew louder that Skip would compete again. Others said he was really through, finally done with contest surfing. Loyal followers of Skip's wet career said he would paddle out again wearing a numbered jersey. The detractors said he had gone too far out into his own thing—and Skip said, "People like to talk, to gossip. It's as natural as breathing in this sport. Rumors travel up and down the surf grapevine faster than by telephone." Frye then admitted, "I'm still going to compete. I'll be entering every contest I can."

There's a special thing happening to surfing, Skip believes. He feels, "This is the creative era, and people—and surfers—are becoming motivated on their own, regardless of commercial stimulation. Contributions to surfing are being made in many back yards and garages by surfers who several years ago wouldn't have thought of trying to build something new. Before they'd have bought their name-surfer wonder model and been satisfied with it. Now it's different. Today there are many one-man gypsy shapers designing, cutting and glassing their own ideas of what a board should be—and surfing will grow and profit because of these lone individuals.

"The new creative attitude among the people involved in surfing today is amazing. Somebody comes up with an idea, and the next week five people in various surfing spots have tried it out—and they become deeply involved in the process of evaluation."

Skip draws rapid sketches in the air to illustrate some

A dedicated professional, Skip Frye, carves apart a fast wave during one of the many California summer surfing contests. (Leroy Grannis)

of the radical shapes the new "gypsy-shaper" boards have taken:

"Before, just a couple of years ago, a new idea would be dreamed up and discussed endlessly. Then somebody would draw plans, but the paper would be around for months before somebody started board-building. Now the idea gets translated into action fast. Barriers are being broken down, commercial barriers for one thing, under the onslaught of this new communication."

So that people wouldn't misunderstand, Frye added, "When I say commercial barriers I mean individual jealousies between builders. I don't mean the manufacturers stand as barriers themselves. Generally they are quite progressive."

Skip, like others who've made the long flight to Australia, attributes much of the creative surge that has hit surfing to the Aussies. "They were riding, talking, watching and communicating—and when I was there the total interest they showed was remarkable.

"They'd go out, try an idea in the waves, and if it didn't work just right, back to the shops they'd go. The boards would be changed and the Aussies would surf some more, all the time chattering and getting ideas passed back and forth. It's this one factor of communicating that gives them momentum—and their incessant talk crossed the Pacific and is begining to change our attitudes here."

In Skip's early surf schooling he was greatly influenced by Dewey Weber and Phil Edwards. Both surfers were traditionalists and were top men of the old school. "Then Greenough came back from Australia with his mind blown free of all preconceptions and he started a lot of us looking in new directions. Greenough stressed surfing on anything people could ride—mats, belly boards, boats, anything that could capture a wave and slide fast. George designs surfing vehicles. It's as simple as that. Before, we were all driving '49 Fords and then up drives George and he had a new Porsche. And George isn't limited to surfing. He talks on everything from fireplace design to unsinkable boats."

Frye went through the whole mind-expansion chemical scene of the past few years, testing one experience after another. Then came marriage and a more relaxed approach to life. Reflecting on his controversial experiences before marriage, Skip summed it up like this:

"Like many kids, I'd had the standard religious upbringing—of sorts. The stress was on punctual performance of rituals, not any meaning in the religious experience, but still you're left with that feeling in the back of your mind that there must be some meaning to life.

"It doesn't take long to realize that this kind of institutionalized religion is a dead, non-vibrant thing—at least it seemed that way to me. And once I got this way I began to feel empty places—that's how the chemicals and I got going. They were promising an instant religious experience, soul and a lot of marvelous revelations.

"I had my bummers—and with the bummers came certain realizations, meaningful realizations and awarenesses. I had to look deeper then, to get out of this man- and laboratory-made happening. The chemicals are like cars, buildings, airplanes—they're not natural. They weren't pushing my realization button.

"Surfing was what seemed always the most meaningful for me. It turned me on the most. I had no bad vibrational feelings from it in any way, and so I left the chemicals and turned back to a natural medium—and that proved to be the final thing, the ultimate actuality—simple acceptance of natural things.

"One of the problems with surfers and people in general in our society is they're so hemmed in by others they have to turn on unnaturally. I think that's part of what's troubling our society. The city that keeps up so close lets people run off their bad feelings on one another, leaving emotional scars.

"David Nuuhiwa is a good example of what the crowd can do to a guy. He came up so fast and they piled on him so hard, so high that he had to look for a way out. If he didn't get in the water and do it he was—well, he was like a matador, and a matador has to be a crowd pleaser or he's finished. He has to blow the crowd's minds with endless happenings. For sure, David was an overnight happening and they nearly destroyed him."

Skip Frye is no overnight happening. He has endured, succeeded and carried on. Because he went through his

Fred Hemmings (*left*) and Buzzy Trent were two greats of
the many MEN WHO RIDE MOUNTAINS.

(Dixon collection)

own grinder and came out nearly whole, he is able to understand the problems of those, like Nuuhiwa and the others in the public eye. Some surfers couldn't take having their every move watched, every thought and word recorded. Skip doesn't condemn, nor does he react with anger or withdraw. He will endure because he can change, grow, and express what is happening. He is the old guard, and the avant garde—simultaneously.

The competitive surfing scene also includes Hawaii and the big-wave riders of the North Shore. The last two winters of Hawaii's big-surf season have seen a revolution in wave-riding styles. The big-wave riders are now younger —much younger—and are emerging to dominate the North Shore. These surfers are even more aggressive in the waves than the pioneers and extremely conscious of their status in the ranking of big-wave riders.

Most of the hot young big-wave riders are Island boys who grew up in the shadows of Peter Cole, Greg Noll, George Downing and Ricky Grigg. The pioneers were their heroes and showed them the way through the rips and currents and how to position to catch the biggest and best waves. These young men started out with the advantage of youth and a trail to follow.

The Hawaiian faction—and most are still in their teens —now dominates the Island surfing life. Surfers like young Reno Abalero, Eddie Aikau, Jock Sutherland and Jeff Hackman, Ben Aipa (an exception—married and in his mid-twenties) take the big waves just as seriously as did the pioneers. They surf better, however, and the rewards are greater today. Now the Hawaiians are being invited to California, Peru, and Australia to surf the contests. Since most of these surfers grew up by the sea and surfing is such a big part of their life, the sudden publicity given them hasn't thrown the Islanders.

While some mainlanders have turned inward to delve into the mystique of surfing, the Hawaiians don't bother. They just concentrate on surfing well. Ben Aipa, for example, works to support a family and still finds time to practice wave-riding daily. He enters every contest he can reach and has climbed to the top ranks of big-wave riders.

The Hawaiians and the Aussies have together advanced

surfing the next step beyond the cultish happenings that still abound along the California coast. They have almost brought surfing back to the basics—back to the clean and simple sport it essentially is.

Surfing grows up, and it appears that maturity has arrived at last. Helping surfing grow from the fads and cults are the very young who look over the heads of the hung-ups with their bag of artificial tricks. The young Hawaiians and Australians and the third generation of California surfers haven't time to turn inward; they've got to be out on the waves surfing and filling themselves with the real mystique of the sport—a fast free ride on the biggest waves that the sea and nature can give them.

CHAPTER 11

The New Wave

Surfing, that amazing, full-blown, around-the-world wet happening stays with us and grows and grows. Some see the expansion of surfing over the past ten years as an expression of both a creative and an escapist need among young people. Others have viewed surfing as an extension of certain societies that have money and time for leisure activities.

The surfing people, if they can be grouped, are a special crowd. The sea that makes their sport possible brings out all sorts of artistic and psychological manifestations among the board riders.

In general, most of those bitten by the surf bug take the trouble to start wondering what their wet adventure is all about. Many surfers try to recapture their wave experiences on paper and on film, or by creating new and better surfboards. The surf writers and surf cameramen are trying desperately to bring the meaning and thrill of wave-riding to the public. A few surfers have gone poetic and penned verse, both free and conventional. Some artists have painted and sketched the experience. The board builders are the sculptors of the sport.

The essential beauty, the visual impact of surfing brings forth an artistic and creative urge not found among the followers of any other sport. Perhaps it's the youth and the young of surfing. Perhaps it's the closeness to nature or the sudden growth of the surfing image that has drawn so many to think of and react to the waves. Not many in the hot rod, sports car, sky rocketing and skin diving, or even the hunting and fishing fraternity, have been inspired to lyric outpourings about their sport.

The surfing scene has also drawn its share of "long-hairs"—the social protesters and, to a lesser extent, the drug users. In the last three years a whole new young group of "far out" surfers have emerged. These are the so-called hippy surfers who delve into the mystique of the psychedelic. A few of these cultists are big-wave riders, most slash apart the smaller, less demanding waves of California and the Atlantic Coast, and a few are exploited puppets of the board- and surf-products manufacturers.

Along the Maui coast, from Malibu and down to Wind and Sea, between Florida and New Jersey, the hippies of the surfing world are following their thing, their bag of tricks that include a liberal use of marijuana and to a limited extent the more powerful chemicals.

The use of pot and chemicals has *not* become widespread among surfers, but enough of the group turn on regularly to have some influence on the nonusers and the sport itself.

The surf magazines and the elders of the sport have tried to play down the extent to which pot and chemicals are used and have editorialized extensively. No statistics are available because the legal aspect of the problem also means that much of what goes on is kept "cool," undercover, out of sight, and away from the attention of the law.

The attraction to pot and the chemicals may be waning. Bob McTavish of Australia states bluntly: "The drug thing went through Australia fast, a few took a taste, found the experience interesting at best and then went back to surfing." Maybe the Aussies aren't as hung-up as their counterparts in the United States.

The dropouts of the surfing scene have found their habitat not in San Francisco but in the backwoods of Maui; near Lahaina, out in the country where the locals and the law seldom bother to investigate live, surfing hippies. This tribe—and they are a tribe in the truest sense—have attempted to return to nature. Some are food faddists living on a macrobiotic diet spiced with crumbled marijuana leaves. Beyond even this group are the true mind blowers so high on chemicals they are actually destroying themselves.

A few of Maui's hippy colony are surfers. Some of the board riders just visit for awhile, then return to the conventional life. A few have stayed and gone on bad bummers. Some believe they've found the answer by going primitive. A few are building boards out of balsa again—feeling that a return to the "natural" materials of surfing will enhance their ability, and their identity with nature. At best the Maui scene is harmless, at worst it destroys people in both mind and body.

The hippie scene on Maui shows the extreme side. What about the other sides of surfing's New Wave?

Surfing has rapidly changed from being an over-socialized "in" activity of the middle class, to become a serious sport. The serious surfers are the pros, the progressive board builders, and the lone "gypsy shapers" who are out to conquer new frontiers of wave-riding.

Bob McTavish, Greenough, and Cooper are examples of dedicated surfers who live and breathe new life into the sport. Dick Brewer in Hawaii, an old-timer and respected board builder, has gone progressive and now builds some of the most radical boards afloat.

The majors of the board-building industry—Con, Hobie, Morey-Pope, Hansen, Yater and a few others—are all beginning to realize that, like Detroit, they must continue to innovate and show some sort of design development. The more progressive board builders hire the best of the new-wave surfers to act as consultants. Cooper advises Morey-Pope and shapes for Yater. Corky Carroll works for Hobie. Another example of a foot-loose one-man international board designer-builder is Peter Coggan of New Zealand.

Peter and a friend carved out a trio of radical short boards back in their home island, fiberglassed them to perfection and set off for America. They found a freighter heading for British Columbia and worked their way across the Pacific chipping paint from her rusting deck plates. In Canada they bought an old car and started down the West Coast for a surfer's grand tour of California surfboard shops.

With their design ideas and their advanced models, Coggan hoped to show the West Coast board manufacturers what was going on across the sea—and at the same time to land themselves a job as surf consultants to support their visit to America.

The current short-board craze shows how rapidly innovation sweeps across the surfing world. On New Years Day, 1968, there were not more than half a dozen of the short vee- or pin-tailed mini-model boards in the whole of California. A few had shown up in Hawaii, flown in by visiting Australians. By mid-year 1968, the board builders were turning out thousands of the short designs. The long ocean-following Pacific Coast Highway of Oregon and California was almost jammed with cars carrying short boards on their roof racks. Suddenly anything over nine feet was obsolete.

The better surf-film makers, the cameramen who really care about the sport, are still out filming and trying to make a better *Endless Summer*. The movie-making team of Greg MacGillivary and Jim Freeman, who produced the artistic and financially successful *Free and Easy*, are at work on a new venture.

Together, MacGillivary and Freeman are attempting to film the dual nature of surfing—excitement and beauty—in a creative, modern way. Their new film has taken them on extensive side trips to South America and Europe as well as to the standard locations of Hawaii and California.

MacGillivary and Freeman want to make the big time with their coming movie; their new film will, like *Endless Summer*, excite a new generation of surfers and draw thousands more to the waves.

So it goes around the world; surfing is here and now and will continue into the future. It's a big wet event and growing bigger. Surfing encompasses all the diverse elements that are drawn to the sport and has yet to be corrupted. How can a wave be corrupted? It can't.

When all the gloss, tissue and verbiage are peeled away, surfing is still the man on his board and the wave. When the giant waves of the North Shore, or Australia's Southern Coast, or South Africa's Indian Ocean, or Peru's Pacific come rolling in fast and tall, the few men who are there to ride will show what surfing is all about. They'll be out in the surf, so fragile against all that power, and paddling down the face trying to make the wave. Some will rise to their feet. Others will fall and be blasted. Most will paddle in exhausted, yet stronger and better for the experience.

No matter what direction surfing takes, the waves will always be the same pure wet moving mountains, always arriving and breaking for the men who paddle out to ride them.